Contents

About the author   v

Introduction   1

1. Myths and facts   4

2. Legal degrees and professional qualifications   10

3. The legal profession   16

4. Finance   31

5. The Civil Service, local government and administration   42

6. Personnel or human resources   54

7. Library and information management   58

8. Information technology   62

9. Journalism and publishing   68

10. Advertising and marketing   76

11. Retail   82

12. Social work and the probation service   87

13. Police and prison services   95

14. The beginning not the end   102

15. Useful addresses   108

What can I do with … a law degree?
This first edition published in 2002 by Trotman and Company Ltd
2 The Green, Richmond, Surrey TW9 1PL

© Trotman and Company Limited 2002

The HESA data quoted in this publication is from the HESA Student
Record July 2000; © Higher Education Statistics Agency Limited
2001.

The Higher Education Statistics Agency (HESA) does not accept any
responsibility for any inferences or conclusions derived from the
data quoted in this publication by third parties.

British Library Cataloguing in Publication Data
A catalogue record for this book is available from the British Library

ISBN 0 85660 852 1

Typeset by Mac Style Ltd, Scarborough, N. Yorkshire

Printed and bound in Great Britain by Creative Print and Design
(Wales) Ltd

About the author

Margaret McAlpine taught for a number of years in schools and colleges in the Midlands and East Anglia, before becoming a journalist. Today she writes for a variety of publications and has a particular interest in writing careers materials for young people. She has three grown-up children and lives with her husband in Suffolk.

'A law degree is an extremely marketable commodity. Law graduates are much sought after by employers in many different sectors because of the disciplines they have gained from undertaking and completing an intensive course of legal study.

'These skills include problem solving and an attention to detail, and these qualities make them an asset to any organisation.'

**Mark Winter, Senior Director,
Group Treasury, Barclays Bank**

Introduction

What can I do with a law degree?

The answer to this question would seem to be – work as a lawyer.

So why write a book about the jobs you can do with a law degree?

The obvious route for law graduates is into the legal profession, to work as solicitors, barristers, or in Scotland as advocates. Or is it? Research shows that for almost every law graduate who goes into legal work there is one who uses his or her law degree to move into a career that at first glance has little or nothing to do with the law. Look at almost any area of work and the chances are you'll find a law graduate there.

Throughout the book are profiles of law graduates, some of them working in the legal profession, others working in marketing, information technology, public relations, finance, commerce, retail and the media. The aim of this book is to look not only at the jobs that legal graduates are expected to do, but also to consider other jobs, to find out what they involve and how a legal qualification can help you to do them well and enjoy doing them.

Why take a degree in law?

Law is an extremely popular subject. In the year 2000, 19,366 people applied to study first degrees in law in England and Wales and 11,467 were accepted. Typically A and B grades at A-level are necessary for a place. Universities do not specify particular subjects and are equally happy with arts or sciences,

so a law degree frees you to choose whatever combination of
A-levels you wish.

Law is an impressive subject and gaining a place on a law
course demonstrates a high level of intelligence and
commitment. What else does a law degree offer?

Practical, soft or transferable skills

These transferable skills are not related directly to a particular
area of academic knowledge. They are practical qualities,
useful in a great many different situations. Once you have
gained them they are with you for life and are greatly valued
by employers.

They include:

★ communication skills – the ability to explain what you mean
simply and clearly, both in speech and in writing.
★ presentation skills – arranging information and putting it
forward in an informative, interesting way.
★ analytical skills – thinking through a problem logically in
order to reach a workable solution.
★ carrying out independent research – selecting information
from reports, journals and books.
★ team skills – the ability to work as part of a group.
★ leadership skills – having the confidence to take the lead
and take control of a situation.
★ information technology skills – as with the majority of
degree courses, law courses rely increasingly on the use of
computers and computerised information.

Who has a law degree?

Politicians with law degrees include Tony Blair, Jack Straw,
Harriet Harman, David Trimble and Paul Boateng, together
with a large number of MPs.

Former South African leader Nelson Mandela ran a successful legal practice in Johannesburg and Margaret Thatcher, former Prime Minister, is qualified as a barrister. Bill Clinton, former US President, has a degree in law, as do Mary Robinson, first woman President of Ireland, Vladimir Putin, President of Russia and Fidel Castro, Premier of Cuba.

Writers France Fyfield, John Grisham and John Mortimer worked as lawyers and used the knowledge they gained to become successful crime writers.

On a lighter note, television personality Clive Anderson is a barrister and Julius O'Riordan, better known as the Radio 1 DJ Judge Jules or *The Judge*, has a degree in law.

1   Myths and facts

Fact

Gaining a legal qualification is expensive
Studying for a degree in any subject is not cheap. The majority of graduates finish university with debts of around £10,000. In order to make this investment worthwhile you need to do your own research into courses and make sure that the one you select is right for you.

In addition to the cost of a first degree, the postgraduate courses (plus living expenses) associated with qualification as a solicitor or barrister will cost in the region of a further £18,000. While the bulk of this figure might be in the form of a long-term professional loan, it is still a large amount.

Balanced against these costs is the comforting fact that starting salaries for professionally qualified legal graduates can be as much as £28,000 a year, although for this figure you would be looking at top legal firms eager to attract the brightest of newcomers.

Further training at postgraduate level is not limited to law graduates. More and more jobs today involve graduates either in full-time postgraduate courses, which are expensive, or in further training while in employment. The days when a graduate could find a job for life requiring little or no further study have gone for ever. Today lifetime learning is a fact, whatever your qualifications.

Fact

A good law degree is an impressive qualification
Law courses are challenging. Entry requirements are high and people who gain a place on a law course are often seen as high flyers destined for success.

This is true, but is not in itself a reason to study law. If you enjoy reasoning and argument, have a good memory and a fascination for current affairs, law could be just the subject for you. If you are artistic, imaginative and creative, you might find it a little dry.

If you are going to study for a degree you need to choose a subject you like. That way you will enjoy the course, work hard and do well. There is little point in choosing a subject solely because of possible job prospects, or because other people tell you it's the right thing to do.

Myth

A career as a lawyer is more exciting and better paid than most other jobs
Although legal work is interesting and for many people fulfilling, television programmes such as *Ally McBeal, LA Law* and *Kavanagh QC* paint a very unreal picture of the legal profession.

Salary levels compare well with other professions, but are not astronomically high. Graduates working in accountancy and information technology tend to earn more than lawyers and the adventure-filled life of a TV lawyer is based on fiction rather than fact.

Myth

You have to have a law degree to become a lawyer
You do not need a law degree to become a lawyer. Although many students who go on to legal training do have a degree in law, it is possible to become a lawyer with a degree in any subject, or even with no degree at all (see Chapter 2 – Legal degrees and professional qualifications).

What can I do with... a law degree?

Myth

All lawyers work in private practice either in solicitors' offices or in courts of law
There are openings for legal professionals in many different areas. Some work in local and national government advising on different aspects of the law, others in advice centres helping people such as asylum seekers, in commercial and manufacturing organisations and banks and insurance companies. Lawyers are to be found just about everywhere.

Myth

Only barristers are allowed to speak in court
This is not the case. All solicitors can represent clients in county courts, magistrates courts and tribunals, and those who have gained a qualification from the Law Society and are solicitor advocates can represent their clients in crown courts, high courts, the Court of Appeal and the House of Lords.

Myth

The legal profession is dominated by males. It's difficult for women to reach the top
It was 1922 when the first woman solicitor qualified and the first woman was called to the Bar in Britain. In 1965 Mrs Elizabeth Lane became the country's first woman high court judge.

Today the legal profession welcomes women and members of minority ethnic groups. In the year 2000 more women than men graduated with first and upper second class law degrees. In 2001 of the 7595 students who enrolled with the Law Society, 62.3 per cent were women and 21.2 per cent were from ethnic minorities. In the year 2000, 54.7 per cent of newly qualified solicitors were women.

6

Cherie Booth, wife of Tony Blair, is an extremely successful barrister. She came from a working class background, was the first member of her family to go to university and financed herself through her studies. Dame Ann Elizabeth Butler Sloss heads the Family Division of the High Court of Justice and Dame Helena Kennedy is a famous lawyer, broadcaster and author. Solicitor Imran Khan has become a well-known figure through his involvement in high-profile legal cases.

Fact

Different countries have different legal systems
This is true even within the United Kingdom. Scotland has its own legal system and some of its own laws. Instead of having solicitors and barristers, Scotland has solicitors and advocates and legal training in Scotland and Northern Ireland differs slightly from that in England and Wales.

European laws play an increasingly important part in life in the UK and all law degree courses cover European law to some extent. Some courses put major emphasis on European law.

Fact

I need some work experience before deciding on a legal career
You certainly do! The only way to know whether any job, legal or otherwise, is right for you is to get in there and find out for yourself.

It is all too easy to build up a fantasy idea of a job that is completely unreal, and today mistakes can be very expensive.

To find a work experience placement, or the opportunity to shadow a lawyer, talk to your careers teacher, Connexions personal adviser, or contact the personnel or human resources department of an organisation yourself.

From law degree to comedy writer ...

Simon Nicholls
BBC comedy writer

A-levels: English, French, Latin
Degree: LLB, University of East Anglia

'Looking back it took me about a week into my degree course to realise I didn't want to be a lawyer. I was sitting in a lecture on land law and it was such heavy going and so dull!

'So why didn't I leave? The answer is I couldn't be bothered. I still had an idea that a law degree might be useful, which has proved to be true and some parts of the course, such as criminal law with its references to certain juicy cases and tort [civil law], for which we had a very good lecturer, were both interesting and often entertaining.

'I'd never done any work experience with a legal company. My dad's a lawyer specialising in entertainment law and he used to get invited to a lot of showbiz parties, so it seemed like a good idea to enter law. In fact my dad had never been to university. He'd trained at a time when you could do it through working with a legal firm.

'After graduation I sold time-share accommodation from a call centre to earn some money and also did clerical work in legal firms. I wanted to get into radio and television and bought *The Guardian* newspaper every Monday when the media jobs are advertised, looking for anything remotely suitable.

'I applied for a job as a runner on a Jonathan Ross panel show by writing a silly letter revealing my thorough knowledge of TV trivia, and got the job. A runner is the lowest form of life, making tea and coffee, buying sandwiches and doing whatever's needed. At the same time I started writing gags for Jonathan on his Radio 2 show and soon I was getting jokes both on radio and TV.

'I then moved up from runner to freelance researcher with the same company. Each job would last around three months and I would write biographies of the personalities appearing on shows, find amusing clips and also write gags. I worked on *Have I Got News for You?*, *Never Mind the Buzzcocks* and *Room 101*.

'While working freelance I got on well with one of the producers of the company and when a job came up producing comedy at the BBC he encouraged me to apply. Around 600 people applied for two jobs and I'm sure one of the reasons I got an interview was because I was the only person who'd applied with a law degree and they wanted to know why I'd applied for a job with them when I could be earning disgusting amounts of money as a lawyer.

'I've been working on *The News Quiz* and *4 at the Store*, a stand-up comedy show, both on Radio 4. I also have a chance to develop my own ideas and currently I'm working on a series of 15-minute comedy dramas written by Alexei Sayle.

'My law degree has been helpful. A knowledge of copyright law is useful and probably without my degree I wouldn't have the job I have now.'

2 Legal degrees and professional qualifications

How do I choose a law degree?

When opting for a course a number of points need to be considered

★ **Do you want to take a straight law course or would you like to combine law studies with another subject such as a foreign language, economics or accountancy or even a science subject?**
If you want to keep your options as wide open as possible, combined courses can be a very good idea.

★ **Would you like to spend part of your degree course studying at a foreign university?**
Some universities offer students the option of a year abroad studying subjects such as European law, international law and human rights law. Time spent at a foreign university counts towards your final degree.

★ **Do you want to live at home while you study?**
Although being independent is a great experience, staying at home is a much cheaper option.

★ **Do you hanker after the buzz of city life or would you be happier in a relatively small town?**
If you are going to move out of your home area, think carefully about the sort of life you want to lead and the sort of place where you would like to live.

★ **Do you find being part of a large crowd exhilarating or does your confidence blossom when you are in a small group?**
Course sizes vary enormously, so check numbers in the prospectus or ring the university and find out how many people would be on your course.

Approved degree courses

Even if you don't intend to become a lawyer, it is still important to make sure that the law course you choose is recognised by the Law Society and the Inns of Court. Recognition means that if you change your mind and do decide to follow a legal career you have an appropriate first qualification.

To be approved a course needs to include the following seven core subjects:

★ Contract
★ Tort – civil law
★ Criminal law
★ Equity – natural justice
★ European Union law
★ Property law
★ Public law.

In addition to these subjects you will receive training in legal research.

A list of approved courses is given in *The Student's Guide to Qualification as a Solicitor* published by the Law Society (see Chapter 15 – Useful addresses).

How do I become a lawyer?

Lawyers in the UK divide into three groups: barristers (advocates in Scotland), solicitors and legal executives.

Solicitors and legal executives are the first point of contact for most people wanting legal advice. They may be general legal experts or they may specialise in a particular area of law such as employment or family law.

Barristers/advocates offer specialist legal advice and represent clients in court. They are not approached directly by clients, but through solicitors.

Training to be a solicitor

Training is in two stages: academic and vocational.

1. Academic stage

England and Wales

There are three routes into a career as a solicitor:

The law degree route

The main route is to take a law degree (LLB) that is recognised by the Law Society followed by further legal training.

No particular A-level subjects are required for a place on a law course and science subjects are as acceptable as arts subjects. However, competition for places is strong and good A-level grades are required.

The non-law degree route

Graduates with a first degree (BA or BSc) in any subject can take a course leading to the Graduate Diploma in Law before going on to further legal training. These are known as conversion courses and they bring graduates up to the standard required to begin legal training. They are offered by institutions across the UK. Some courses are run on a part-time basis and by distance learning, so it is possible to study while supporting yourself in a job. The minimum entry qualification is usually a lower second class honours degree.

The non-graduate route

It is possible to become a solicitor without having a degree by following the Institute of Legal Executives (ILEX) or legal training route. Training is usually carried out on a part-time basis while working with a legal firm although some colleges do run full-time courses.

To become a Member (MILEX) you need to pass:

Professional Diplomas in Law
- Level 3 Professional Diploma in Law (A-level standard)
- Level 4 Professional Higher Diploma in Law (degree standard).

Legal executives, who have passed the MILEX exams, have five years' legal experience and are over 25 years old, are eligible to apply for a place on a Legal Practice Course to train as a solicitor.

Scotland
The routes to qualification are through an approved law degree (LLB) course at a Scottish university or by undertaking a three-year pre-Diploma traineeship and sitting the Law Society examinations. Graduates with a degree in a subject other than law can take an accelerated law degree course and gain an ordinary degree in two years and an honours degree in three years.

Northern Ireland
Graduates with a degree in a subject other than law need to show the Law Society of Northern Ireland that they have a satisfactory level of legal knowledge. The way to do this is by taking the Bachelor of Legal Science degree at Queen's University Belfast. This is a conversion course lasting two years full time and from three to five years part time.

Anyone over the age of 29 years who has been employed in a solicitor's practice for seven years and can satisfy the Law Society of Northern Ireland that he or she has gained the necessary knowledge and experience can begin training as a solicitor.

2. *Vocational stage*

Once the academic stage is completed, students move on to the vocational stage.

England and Wales
The first stage of vocational training is the Legal Practice
Course, which is one year full time and two years part time
and is run at institutions across the country.

The Legal Practice Course is followed by the Training
Contract. Trainees are attached to qualified solicitors who
advise and guide them while monitoring their progress. The
Training Contract usually lasts two years and during that time
trainees must also complete the Professional Skills Course,
which is a short course covering financial and business skills,
advocacy and communication skills and client care and
professional standards.

The number of students seeking Training Contracts is greater
than the number of contracts available. Figures produced by
the Law Society together with the University of Sheffield
revealed that in the year 1999–2000 there were 5800 students
seeking Training Contracts and 4700 contracts being offered,
so 1100 students were disappointed.

Scotland
After gaining a law degree, trainees take a Postgraduate
Diploma in Legal Practice at a Scottish university followed by a
two-year traineeship overseen by the Law Society of Scotland.

Northern Ireland
Solicitor training is known as apprenticeship and involves work
in a solicitor's office under a master who is a qualified solicitor
and block release at the Institute of Professional Legal Studies.
An apprenticeship lasts two years for postgraduate trainees
and four years for trainees who do not have a degree.

Training to be a barrister/advocate

The non-graduate entry route is not open to
barristers/advocates. Entrants need a law degree or a non-law
degree plus a law conversion qualification.

England and Wales
Before vocational training begins a student must become a member of one of the Inns of Court. There are four of them, all based in London: Lincoln's Inn, Inner Temple, Middle Temple and Gray's Inn. These give support to student members including mentoring and guidance from qualified barristers and also offer bursaries and scholarships.

All barristers have to complete a one-year full-time or two-year part-time Bar Vocational Course that includes role-playing exercises and acting out court procedures as well as academic subjects. After BVC training students have to complete pupillage, which is a year's training with six months spent shadowing an experienced barrister and the rest carrying out work under supervision.

Scotland
Trainee advocates are called intrants and they take the full-time Diploma in Legal Practice Course as trainee solicitors. Following this they train for 21 months in a solicitor's office for which they receive a salary. The final stage of training is nine months of pupillage known as 'devilling' spent with a member of the Scottish Bar. During this time they must pass the Faculty of Advocates exams for which there are no formal lecture courses.

Northern Ireland
Students wishing to become barristers in Northern Ireland must take the competitive exam for a place on the vocational course run by the Institute of Professional Legal Studies. There are only 25 places a year and around 350 applicants. This is followed by six months' pupillage under a barrister before a pupil receives a Practising Certificate and becomes a barrister.

3 The legal profession

Solicitor

In the year 2000, 24 per cent of households in England and Wales sought legal advice from a solicitor. The most common reasons for this were buying a house, claiming compensation, making a will or getting divorced. Statistics suggest the majority of these people thought they received good advice from their solicitor and were pleased with the service.

Main areas of work

Business and Commercial Law involves drawing up contracts, tax and VAT legislation, employment law, patents (the protection of new ideas), export law and the sale of companies. Some companies have their own legal departments but use outside solicitors when they need them.

Probate is work connected with wills: helping people to make them, making sure their instructions are carried out, looking after property and estates after their death and dealing with people's affairs when they die without making a will.

Conveyancing is the legal side of buying and selling property – finding out information that might affect the buyers, such as the boundaries between a property and neighbouring houses and future plans for building in the area, followed by drawing up a contract of sale.

Litigation involves advising clients who are in dispute or disagreement with other people. This work falls into two groups:

Criminal law covers crimes or public wrongs that are punishable by the state – such as murder, robbery or fraud.

Civil law includes all other cases where individuals or businesses are in dispute about a situation, for example personal injury or negligence.

If the case comes to court the solicitor can represent the client in either the magistrates court or the county court. More serious criminal cases are heard in the crown court where a solicitor will normally brief a barrister to speak in court for the client.

Where do solicitors work?

Private practice

Nearly 80 per cent of solicitors work in private practice. This is a legal practice set up to advise clients including individuals, businesses, charities or government departments.

Some solicitors work alone, in single person practices, or work with other solicitors. The size of these practices varies from two or three solicitors to huge firms. In small practices solicitors tend to offer advice on a range of subjects, while in larger practices they are likely to specialise.

By no means do all solicitors work in private practice. There are good employment opportunities for solicitors in the following areas:

Industry and commerce

Solicitors are employed by a company, often a large multinational organisation, to deal solely with that company's legal affairs. Their work concerns the legal implications of decisions made by the company, for example mergers, contracts, health and safety and employment matters.

Local authorities

County councils, borough councils and district councils employ solicitors to advise them on the laws affecting a wide range of areas such as childcare, licensing applications and planning.

17

Central government

Solicitors working in government frequently advise ministers and administrators on the law and the issues relating to the particular responsibilities covered by their department. The topics are extremely wide and often at the forefront of legal thinking. Other government lawyers carry out the more 'usual' practices of solicitors such as conveyancing and will making – especially where people do not have the maturity or physical or mental ability to represent themselves.

Crown Prosecution Service (Procurator Fiscal Service in Scotland)

When individuals appear in court to answer a charge the prosecution is undertaken by the Crown Prosecution Service (Procurator Fiscal Service) and the defence by lawyers in private practice.

Solicitors in the CPS advise the police on whether or not there is enough evidence to bring a prosecution case, based on the amount of evidence against an individual. When the decision is made to prosecute, the case is prepared by solicitors working in the CPS.

Charities

There are a limited number of opportunities for solicitors to work with charities. With some organisations, such as those working with homeless people or those with mental health problems, the work can involve giving legal advice to individuals. If the charity is raising money for developing countries the work is likely to be the examination of legal issues that affect the charity.

The Army Legal Service

This is part of the Adjutant General's Corps. It is officer entry only and has opportunities particularly for solicitors specialising in military law.

Sonia Sharp
Solicitor specialising in licensing law

A-levels: English literature, French, maths
Degree: LLB, Essex Institute (now Anglia Polytechnic University)
          Legal Practice Course, Chester Law School

'I was 11 when I decided I wanted to be a lawyer. Such an early decision does have its drawbacks, but it meant I had plenty of opportunity for work experience in solicitors' offices and in local government.'

Despite winning the Sweet & Maxwell Mooting Prize for Inner London at university, which could have suggested a career as a barrister, Sonia decided to become a solicitor. During her Legal Practice Course at Chester she arranged articles for herself with a medium-sized firm in East Anglia, before taking a year out to travel the world.

In 1992 a recession was gripping the UK and neither Sonia nor the firm's other trainee was offered a permanent post. She found a job with another legal firm, only to be made redundant within six months. Back in the job market, Sonia had four offers and took the job of setting up a matrimonial department in a small private practice.

Looking back she says, 'It was a steep learning curve and possibly too soon in my career for that sort of challenge. I found the constant pressure to bring in fees quite stressful. Most of the work was legally aided, which also meant a long wait for payment. After a couple of years I left and took a job in local government as assistant solicitor with a district council.

'Local government work is varied and interesting. Our department provided general legal advice to all internal staff. My main areas of work were planning and environmental law. I dealt with planning applications, attended committee meetings and gave advice to officers and elected counsellors on contentious or difficult issues. I also dealt with public entertainment licences and taxi licences.

'My next move was as a solicitor with a neighbouring borough council where I had more responsibility. I ran training courses for counsellors, did court enforcement work that meant preparing and taking cases to court and acting as advocate or prosecutor in the magistrates court on behalf of the council.

'After a number of years in local government I took the plunge and returned to private practice. I'm now an associate solicitor in the environmental, licensing and planning department of a legal firm with around 150 staff.

'My clients are nightclub and restaurant owners, pub managers and tenants and breweries wanting liquor licences or public entertainment licences. I travel a great deal with my job and meet a lot of people, which I enjoy.

'The challenge of my job often lies in the sheer volume of work, which means I need time management skills and the ability to prioritise.'

Eleanor Robinson
Solicitor, Legal Advisers Branch, The Home Office

A-levels: English, history, Latin
Degree: BA English, Oxford University
Common Professional Examination (Conversion Course) and Legal Practice Course, York College of Law

'I read English at university, which I feel gave me additional breadth and flexibility when considering a career. From Oxford I went to York College of Law where I took a legal conversion course followed by the Legal Practice Course.

'The fascinating point about the law is that it's constantly changing. There is always something new, which has all sorts of implications in different areas. Law makes you think in a disciplined way and develops lots of different skills. You learn to express your point of view, to listen to other people, to negotiate and to work with them. The important point about these skills is that they are useful whatever you do, in any career and in your personal life.

'On finishing my legal studies I went with some friends to South America where I spent three months travelling and three months teaching English to people with disabilities in a Leonard Cheshire home.

'Back in London I became a trainee solicitor in private practice. On qualifying I joined the intellectual property department, dealing mainly with trademarks and patents. Then I opted for a complete culture change and joined the Legal Advisers Branch of the Home Office in the European Union and Immigration team.

'That's one of the great things about law – the transferable skills you gain mean you can move from one area of work to another without too many problems.

'My work with the Home Office involves advising on rights of entry and residence for EEA nationals and I have attended the European Court of Justice in Luxembourg as well as the Commission in Brussels. At present I'm part of a team working on a new Immigration Bill, making sure it complies with rulings made by the courts.

'I also have to look at the implications of possible legislation in the light of the Human Rights Act. This recognises basic human rights such as the right to family life, the right not to suffer inhumane treatment and the right to a fair trial. The Human Rights Act brought the European Convention of Human Rights (which was drawn up in 1951, largely in response to human suffering in World War Two) within the UK system of law in 2000. This means that the British government must act in compliance with it.

'At present I have no thoughts of moving departments, but it isn't difficult to transfer from one to another within the Home Office or government as a whole.'

Joss Saunders
Legal Adviser and Company Secretary, Oxfam

A-levels: French, German, history
Degree: BA History, Oxford University
Conversion Course and Legal Practice Course, City of London Polytechnic (now London Metropolitan University)

'To be a lawyer with a charity you need first to be good at your job and, secondly, you have to be enthusiastic about the aims of the organisation.'

This is the advice given by Joss Saunders, Legal Adviser and Company Secretary to Oxfam. He also points out that there are not a great many openings for solicitors with charities, and those there are pay significantly less than other areas of legal work. However, as far as Joss is concerned his job is high in satisfaction.

Oxfam has two branches of work. One is emergency relief in areas stricken by natural disasters or war, the other is long-term development work. It is the second area in which Joss is more deeply involved.

Over the past few months Joss has been working on ensuring that Oxfam's new *Make Trade Fair* website complied with the Internet rules and he is responsible for registering Oxfam in countries such as Equador and Tajikistan where new programmes have just started.

A major challenge he faces is that field workers operate in countries with their own legal systems. For example, he recently received a phone call from staff in Kosovo about to make a significant purchase, asking for a draft contract to be drawn up within the hour.

Joss is now establishing a database, recording laws in different countries that could affect Oxfam staff. When it's complete he intends to make the database available to other charities.

Joss's career path was in itself unusual. He explains: 'I read history at university and after graduation did voluntary work in Uganda, teaching and building water tanks. I then did my legal training at the City of London Polytechnic, which I chose because it wasn't exclusively a law school and I wanted to mix with people other than lawyers.'

The next two years were spent working in commercial litigation, until Joss's wife's job took them to Poland, where he lectured in law. The Prince of Wales on an official visit to Poland asked Joss to set up a branch of his charity, the Prince of Wales Business Leaders Forum.

On their return to the UK the couple moved to Oxford and Joss's original plan was to work part time for a private practice and do voluntary work for Oxfam. However the legal firm for which he worked did work for Oxfam. After a while Joss was seconded to Oxfam by his firm and eventually went to work full time for the charity.

He sees work for Oxfam as different from legal work with some other charities, because 'Oxfam works in disaster areas and in developing countries, so I don't actually meet the people we help. In charities running law centres or working in areas such as homelessness and mental health, lawyers probably spend some of their time giving advice to people with problems.'

Despite the differences there are, he feels, similarities in all charity work. 'What they have in common is the enthusiasm and commitment of the staff.'

Barrister

Barristers are specialist legal advisers trained to provide independent legal advice to clients on the strengths and weaknesses of their case. Under what is known as the 'Cab Rank Rule' if a barrister is available to act on someone's behalf he or she must take the case. When a case comes to trial in a civil or a criminal court, barristers present the case and cross-examine witnesses.

Most barristers are self-employed, although some are employed by organisations, including government departments, which use the legal skills that barristers have in a similar way to solicitors. Government barristers also prosecute on behalf of their department, for example tax fraud or drug smuggling. The Crown Prosecution Service (CPS), as its name suggests, prosecutes criminal cases on behalf of the Crown. However the CPS and the government also employ barristers from the independent bar.

QCs are senior barristers of outstanding ability who are instructed in very serious or complex cases.

Rachel Crasnow
Barrister, Cloister Chambers, The Temple, Inns of Court, London

A-levels: English, maths, history
Degree: BA English, Oxford University
Conversion course, Graduate Diploma in Law, City University London
Bar Vocational Course (BVC) The Inns of Court School of Law

When Rachel started her degree course at 19 she had no plans for a legal career and admits 'I didn't know the difference between a barrister and a solicitor!'

In her last year at Oxford she had a week's work experience with a barrister, called a mini-pupillage, which gave her an insight into what the job entailed, and she decided to try a legal career.

However Rachel is still pleased that she studied English at university. 'My advice to anyone is: don't make decisions too early and never embark on a career without work experience to see what the job is really like. It may be more expensive to do a conversion course after a first degree, rather than a law degree in the first place, but I gained a great deal from studying English and I don't feel I missed out by not studying for a degree in law.'

She continues: 'I was lucky in finding a traineeship – called a pupillage – as it is very competitive. By that time I had quite a lot of legal work experience, including working in a solicitor's office. Today there is a central system, similar to UCAS, to which people apply, but it still isn't easy.'

Pupils have to do 12 months' minimum of pupillage, at one or more chambers. Once trainee barristers have completed their pupillage there is less than a 50 per cent chance they will be kept on by their chambers. In Rachel's case, her second training chambers offered her a permanent place.

Barristers are self-employed and pay a fee to their chambers to cover staff salaries, rent of their buildings and use of facilities. Newly qualified barristers have to establish themselves, which isn't easy. They rely on their clerks to get them work, as well as on the reputation of their chambers.

Rachel explains, 'When solicitors ring and ask for a junior barrister it is the clerks of the chambers who allocate the work. The hope is that if the work is done well the solicitors might ask for that barrister by name the next time.

'The Cab Rank Rule means that if barristers are free and offered work they must take it, if they are competent to do it. If they are not available the clerks will suggest someone else. This is another way a newly qualified barrister is given work.'

To be a barrister, in Rachel's words, 'You need to be stubborn and tenacious, especially in the early years.'

She specialises in employment and discrimination law and travels all over the country. For her the best part of the job is the variety of people she meets, the advocacy and the challenge of diverse legal arguments.

Her advice to anyone considering a career as a barrister is, 'You need to be a good communicator, have good self-management skills and plenty of energy.'

Legal executive

In many ways the work of legal executives is similar to that of solicitors. They work on cases before they come to court, interview and advise clients, draw up wills and property and sales agreements, help barristers and solicitors to present cases in court. They also represent clients in court in civil cases.

Legal executives cannot become partners in a legal practice, but they do undertake much of the practical and technical work in a solicitor's office. In some firms they are practice managers, giving work to junior staff, supervising clerks and secretaries and taking charge of accounts.

You don't have to have a law degree or any degree at all to train as a legal executive (see Chapter 2 – Legal degrees and professional qualifications). However, graduates with a law degree may be exempt from the academic elements of the professional qualifications in law of the Institute of Legal Executives (ILEX). They go straight to studying on the Legal Practice Course, usually on a part-time basis while working in a legal environment. It takes around 12 months for law graduates to complete the course. They then have to work in legal employment for five years before qualifying as a legal executive. During this time they are earning a salary and gaining practical experience.

Some legal executives with law degrees choose to remain working as legal executives while others go on to qualify as solicitors. Around 15 per cent of students who register with ILEX have studied to degree level and about half of these have a degree in law.

Judy Banyard
Litigation Manager, Beynon Khang

A-levels: English, sociology
Degree: BA Law, Leicester Polytechnic (now De Montfort University)
Fellow of the Institute of Legal Executives

Judy's responsibilities include IT systems and general management duties. In addition she has her own legal caseload of matrimonial law, wills and probate cases.

Beynon Khang is a small legal practice based in Birmingham, specialising in preparing serious fraud cases for court. In addition to her administration duties and general legal work, Judy works as part of the defence team on fraud cases, checking proofs of evidence from clients and obtaining their instructions in respect of evidence against them, going over papers and preparing reports and schedules.

She attends court, sitting behind the barrister who is representing her client, acting as the contact between the two of them and making sure all the necessary documents are in court.

Court hearings are held in the area where the crime was committed so Judy's job takes her all over the country. As fraud cases are often long and complicated this can mean a fair amount of travel over quite long periods and occasional stays away from home.

In matrimonial cases, which are heard in the Family Division of the county court, Judy represents her client in court by presenting her client's case and answering questions put to her by the district judge.

When Judy was at school she had no thoughts of a legal career. She explains, 'I trained as a nursery nurse and worked in a nursery until my first child was born.

'When my two children were young my husband brought home details of a four-year part-time law degree at what was then Leicester Polytechnic. He decided against taking the degree, but I read the course details and decided it sounded really interesting. We were living near Leicester at the time and the lectures fitted into my childcare routine.

'By the time I graduated we had moved to Birmingham for my husband's job. I enrolled on the Legal Practice Course to become a solicitor, but failed to qualify at the first attempt. I could have retaken the course, but decided against it.

'I'd given the course everything I could, considering my other commitments. I'd been offered a job with a legal firm, which did not depend on passing the course, and I decided to take it.

'Looking into the ILEX Legal Executive training I found my qualifications exempted me from all but two of the papers. This was a different way of developing a legal career and one that suited me well. The ILEX training was practical, I earned money as I trained and today being a legal executive and not a solicitor doesn't prevent me doing any of the work I enjoy.

'As a legal executive I can't be a partner in a legal practice. Instead I'm the principal fee earner. I could speak in a magistrates court if I took a further qualification, but that isn't an area of work which particularly interests me.

'Today with the ILEX qualification legal executives can train as solicitors, so the old difference between solicitors and legal executives is becoming even less marked. In recent years legal executives have acquired rights of representation in the courts and are in charge of legal departments. Their names are even appearing on firms' letterheads!'

The paralegal option

This is becoming an increasingly attractive option for law graduates who have not been able to find a Training Contract with a solicitor, or who haven't finally decided whether they want a legal career. It involves working with a firm of solicitors on a short-term contract, perhaps for six months or a year, supporting qualified staff in a variety of different ways.

The legal firm benefits from having a member of staff with a legal background, while paralegal employees gain experience, which puts them in a much stronger position should they decide to look for a Training Contract in the future.

The work paralegals do varies, but is likely to involve assisting in background work, carrying out research, drafting legal documents and letters and preparing material for trials. Paralegal staff do not work independently. Everything they do is checked carefully by solicitors, but in most cases they are given interesting work and do not spend their time sticking down envelopes or working the photocopier.

Most legal firms stress that paralegal work does not lead directly to a Training Contract, and some make a point of never offering Training Contacts to paralegal staff. Even so, such jobs are an opportunity to make a positive impression, to gain practical experience and to have a long hard look at whether the work is right for you.

James Viney
Paralegal, Wragge & Co., Birmingham

A-levels: English, Latin, French, general studies
Degree: BA Politics, Exeter University
Conversion Course, Graduate Diploma in Law,
Birmingham University
Legal Practice Course, Birmingham University

James spent 16 months working in a paralegal role at Wragge &
Co., an international, commercial and general legal practice
based in Birmingham.

As a member of the dispute resolution group he gave
professional support to colleagues by investigating and
researching specific legal points. James' interest in IT led him
to take an interest in the firm's knowledge management
system and to organise training sessions for the administration
team.

Looking back on the 16 months he spent doing paralegal work,
James feels: 'I learned a great deal and certainly improved the
level of my time management and client relationship skills.
When I do start my professional training I shall be able to hit the
ground running.'

James now has a training place with another legal practice in
Birmingham.

What can I do with... a law degree?

'Smith & Williamson is a top-tier firm of chartered accountants with an investment management and private banking house.

'We run a graduate programme, employing approximately 35 students per year in a number of professions, predominantly audit and business services, corporate and personal tax and investment management.

'Applications are welcome from graduates from any degree discipline. We are seeking candidates who have strong communication and problem-solving skills, who are able to demonstrate a high level of numeracy, and who have an interest in business and the economy.

'We have recently recruited a number of law graduates into finance careers; in particular, the taxation subjects studied during a law degree have led many disillusioned lawyers into a tax career.'

**Miranda Isherwood, Recruitment Officer,
Smith & Williamson**

Finance 4

Among graduates with a law degree the most popular choice for those who don't go into the legal profession is a career in finance.

Major reasons for this are the career opportunities available and the financial rewards. While legal graduates are the highest earners on starting work, those going into the financial sector go into work immediately after graduation and are paid as they train. Starting salaries for graduates going into the financial sector vary enormously depending upon the training firm. They can be £23,500 and in some cases even higher. Successful graduates in the financial sector can earn immensely high salaries.

A degree in maths or a subject with a high numerical content is not a requirement for a career in finance – in fact only 4 per cent of trainees with the Institute of Chartered Accountants in England and Wales (ICAEW) are accountancy graduates. Employers look for a good degree in any subject and the right type of skills. This is where law graduates can be at a definite advantage, as the soft skills gained through studying law closely match those sought by employers in the financial sector.

Law graduates may apply for credit (to study to become an Associated Chartered Accountant with the ICAEW) providing they have completed the appropriate law modules as part of their studies. Law graduates (either single or joint honours) from the UK or the Republic of Ireland will automatically be awarded credit for both commercial and company law, provided a company law module has been completed.

Skills required in financial work

★ numerical skills – employers often set numeracy tests as part of recruitment interviews
★ analytical skills
★ communication skills
★ flexibility
★ tact and diplomacy
★ good interpersonal skills – ability to get on well with people from different backgrounds
★ ability to work as part of a team
★ leadership skills
★ self-motivation
★ energy and ability to work hard.

These requirements closely match the skills most graduates feel they have gained from a law degree.

Accountancy

Accountants work in industry and commerce and in the public sector. Around half of them work as partners or employees in accountancy firms, or as sole practitioners, offering fee-paying client services ranging from audit and tax to financial management and forensic accounting. Others go into industry and commerce where the opportunities are just as varied. Every business needs a financial guru and qualified accountants are in demand everywhere. Many recruitment agencies start headhunting newly qualified accountants before the official final examination results are out.

The Jobs

Examples of the jobs currently filled by accountants are:

★ Chairman of a leisure and retail group
★ Deputy Chief Executive of an FA Premiership football club
★ Deputy Chairman of a motor manufacturing company.

Accountants also work in the public sector for organisations such as the NHS, the Post Office, universities, housing associations and in central and local government. An increasing number of accountants are taking on roles such as:

★ Director of Finance, NHS Trust
★ Area Accountant at the Inland Revenue
★ Head of Government Accounts at the Treasury.

Professionally qualified accountants are known as either certified or chartered accountants. Their role is to make sure clients of whatever size make best use of their financial resources. They prepare and audit accounts, prepare tax returns, diagnose financial problems, give advice on mergers and corporate finance.

Accounting divides into two main areas: financial and management.

Financial accountants keep financial records, analyse them and prepare the accounts and reports required by law.

Management accountants advise on the financial implications of possible developments, such as expansion into a new area of production, or a merger with another organisation.

Training is provided by a number of professional bodies (see Chapter 15 – Useful addresses), the largest of which is the ICAEW. Training consists of a three-year training contract with an authorised training firm, combining work experience with academic study and examinations.

Jackie Ponting enjoyed her degree course but decided while at university that she wanted a career in accountancy.

What can I do with... a law degree?

Jackie Ponting
Trainee Chartered Accountant, Smith & Williamson Investment Bank

A-levels: maths, English literature and law
Degree: LLB, Sheffield University

Before taking up her place at university, Jackie had a year out to work as an au pair in Germany. This meant that when she arrived at Sheffield she had already lived independently and gained a number of practical skills.

In Jackie's words, 'The children were lovely but looking after them certainly made me realise I didn't want to have a family for a long time! During the 12 months I became quite well organised, which helped me with my studies.

'I thoroughly enjoyed studying law, but decided before the end of the course that I wanted to be an accountant. I looked into taking further legal training and decided it seemed rather dry and tedious! Also I'm ambitious and I liked the idea of being paid to gain a qualification that would improve my job opportunities.

'That is not to say I regret studying law because I certainly don't. The course was challenging and taught me a great deal. There is a massive amount of information to digest on a law course and students have to learn to work quickly. We had to read a large number of cases and articles, extracting and analysing information on the way. A law degree certainly keeps your memory working. This has been helpful in working for my current qualification, as it is a key exam technique.

'I spent my final year in Holland at Nijmegen University. The lectures were in English and the marks I gained there went towards my degree. It was a fantastic experience and a chance to study refugee law and human rights law, as well as international law and comparative criminal laws.

'Knowing I wanted to study accountancy I put my name and details on a careers website on graduation and was contacted by a firm of chartered accountants, with an investment management and private banking house.

'I work in the Audit Department as a trainee chartered accountant. Much of my time is spent outside the office, working on clients' premises carrying out statutory audits, making sure books balance and figures are true and fair.

'The majority of clients are small to medium-sized companies and include non-profit-making organisations such as charities and housing associations. Their size means an audit takes around two to three weeks, whereas with bigger organisations it could take several months. I enjoy change and meeting new people, so moving on suits me well.

'Accountancy today is less about adding up figures than understanding them, recognising any trends that occur and using them in planning new strategies. It is a higher level of work than simply number crunching.

'I'm not sure about the future. I suppose I might one day go back and do some legal training, but that's not very likely. One possibility is to join the finance department of a legal partnership!'

Michael Catterall spent several years working as a barrister before coming to the conclusion that for a number of reasons he was better suited to a career in accountancy. He now works as a tax consultant in the north of England.

Michael Catterall
Corporate Tax Consultant

A-levels: English literature, history, chemistry
Degree: BA Law, Oxford University
        Bar Vocational Course (BVC), Inns of Court Law
        School

With hindsight Michael can see that his choice of A-levels reflected a pull between arts subjects and science.

After training as a barrister he joined a set of chambers that, while it dealt with a range of cases, did have a focus on crime. This meant the majority of Michael's work was with criminal cases.

In his words, 'I soon realised that commercial legal work would probably have suited me better, but commercial law is a popular area and a decision to specialise in it needs to be made at university.

'I found my work as a barrister was sometimes quite lonely. Barristers are self-employed, which means that, especially in the early days, we often have to work alone. I would travel to court, meet my client, who might well prove difficult, and be required to defend him or her against the CPS lawyer.

'Constantly travelling to different places around the country, appearing before different magistrates and judges, and having to deal with a new client on an almost daily basis meant that the job could sometimes feel isolating.

'Although I'm an independent person I started to feel that I would like a support structure within my job and the chance to work as part of a team. I began to think of other options beyond a legal career.

'Accountancy appealed to me because it offered on-the-job training and I didn't want to go back to being a student. I felt that my commercial knowledge would benefit from accountancy training and would complement the legal abilities I had already developed.

'Taxation work has become the mainstay of the accountancy profession and there are significant elements of law attached to it, so it suits me well.

'My legal training is certainly a help to me. Not only has it given me a bank of knowledge to which I can refer, it also enables me to interpret complex ideas for my clients.'

Banking

In recent years banks have started to offer customers a wide range of services including foreign exchange services, mortgages, insurance and financial advice. Today banks, insurance companies, building societies and supermarkets all offer similar services.

Banks provide a wealth of career opportunities and welcome applications from legal graduates. Many banks run accelerated or fast-track programmes for graduates, designed to give experience of the range of work.

Professional qualifications are awarded by the Institute of Financial Services (IFS), which is the official body of the Chartered Institute of Bankers (CIB) (see Chapter 15 – Useful addresses). The institute provides a range of qualifications including the BSc (Hons) in Financial Services and Associateship. It also offers a range of regulatory qualifications such as the Certificate for Financial Advisers and the Certificate in Mortgage Advice and Practice.

The Bank of England acts as banker to the government and other UK banks. It advises the Treasury, raises finance and issues bank notes. It has a training scheme open to graduates with any degree, which is known as the Trainee Officials Programme.

Retail banks look after the accounts of personal and business customers. They include the well-known high street names such as Lloyds TSB, Barclays, NatWest, plus a number of former building societies such as the Abbey National, Bristol & West and Halifax.

Investment or merchant banks provide banking for companies, governments and a small group of extremely wealthy people.

The jobs

It is impossible to cover all the opportunities available in the banking sector. What follows are just some examples.

A bank manager is in charge of the day-to-day running of a branch, making sure it runs efficiently, that staff are motivated and well trained and that premises are secure. A manager makes decisions about lending money, gives customers financial advice, reviews and approves overdrafts and establishes good relationships with local businesses.

An investment adviser monitors the stock market and other trends that affect investments and advises customers on their investments, acts on customers' instructions, arranges for buying and selling of shares and promotes other services provided by the bank.

An investment banker works with corporate and government clients providing long-term financial advice, including raising capital, undertaking mergers and privatisations. The work involves close contact with clients, accountants and lawyers. Investment banks, the Bank of England, the London Stock Exchange and venture capital firms all offer employment opportunities to investment bankers.

A credit analyst deals with requests for credit, assessing the risks involved. Such requests can be enormous, for example when a company requests a loan of £10 million to purchase new machinery.

For Mark Winter the move from a legal career to one in finance was a gradual process.

Mark Winter
Senior Director, Group Treasury, Barclays Bank

A-levels: sociology, politics and government
Degree: BA Law, City of London Polytechnic (now Guildhall University)
Bar Vocational Course (BVC), Inns of Court School of Law.

After taking A-levels Mark studied for a degree in law and went on to train as a barrister.

Having completed his BVC training he found himself unable to continue as a barrister due to financial pressures and the need to earn some money quickly. He took up temporary work, which was usually in the back office of banks, and as he says himself, 'had nothing to do with the law'.

One merchant bank where he was working did not have its own legal department, and when senior staff realised that Mark was a lawyer they began to give him commercial contracts to check through. Almost before he knew it he was back working in the legal field.

After nine months Mark moved to the Property Department of United Dominions Limited, drawing up and checking documents for property loans, and he remained there for three years. His next move was as a lawyer to a company in the field of securitisation (off-balance sheet funding of loans assets).

According to Mark his next job, which was with Barclays Bank, 'marked the point at which I stopped being a lawyer and became a banker'. Based at the bank's headquarters in London, the legal aspect of his work was now undertaken by lawyers from the big legal firms in the capital, while Mark helped structure the transactions for the bank.

His move from a legal to a financial career is not, he feels, so unusual. Mark explains: 'There are a great many lawyers to be found in banking and finance. In many ways it's a natural progression and an easy step to take; basically it means becoming involved in the bank's transactions at an earlier, structuring stage.

'The same mental disciplines are needed to work in finance and law: the ability to analyse closely, to have an eye for detail and well-developed problem-solving skills.'

Insurance

Insurance provides financial protection against loss or misfortune. Taking out holiday insurance means if you are taken ill on holiday you will receive medical treatment and if necessary be flown home. If you have to cancel your holiday, you will receive compensation.

Insurance companies work on the principle that while many people will insure themselves against a particular misfortune, such as serious injury, only a few will actually suffer such an injury and make a claim.

Insurance work falls into three main groups:

★ **Life insurance** – insuring people against premature death or permanent injury
★ **General insurance**:
  – Personal – household, motor and accident
  – Commercial – insurance for companies and employees
★ **Reinsurance** – insurers spreading their risks by taking out their own insurance against claims.

The professional body responsible for training in the insurance industry is the Chartered Insurance Institute (CII). (See Chapter 15 – Useful addresses.)

The jobs

A broker finds the best insurance policies for clients, ranging from holiday or car insurance to cover for a new factory for a corporate client. Brokers gather information from clients and put the information into a written report for the underwriters.

At Lloyd's, brokers deal with risks involving millions of pounds and approach underwriters working for syndicates, asking them to accept a proportion of the risk. Most brokers specialise in a particular type of insurance.

An underwriter measures the risk involved in issuing an insurance policy, examining the proposals drawn up by brokers, checking whether the information is correct and whether any further information should be taken into account. Some of the work is routine, such as contacting a doctor to check that the information given for a life insurance policy is correct.

Experienced underwriters are responsible for designing policies for exceptional situations, for example to cover a sporting event involving famous athletes. In these cases they have to examine a great many different factors before writing the policy listing all the liabilities that are accepted and any exceptions which will not be covered.

The Stock Exchange

Bonds are issued by the government when it needs to raise money, while shares are issued by companies to raise capital. When a company is floated on the Stock Exchange directors are selling parts of it to shareholders who share in its profits and losses. Individuals and institutions such as pension funds buy and sell shares and bonds. All such trading is done through the London Stock Exchange or through a stockbroker.

The jobs

A market trader buys and sells shares. The work involves concentrating for long periods, thinking quickly and working under intense pressure. Judgement is based on detailed knowledge of the financial market, which is constantly changing. Before market traders can work on the Stock Exchange they have to pass the Domestic Equity Market Oral Examination run by the Stock Exchange and the Securities Institute.

A stockbroker is paid a commission by clients for advising them on investments on the Stock Exchange. In some cases they have full responsibility for a client's investments and are entrusted to make decisions on their behalf. In other cases they consult the client before buying or selling takes place. This is a high-risk area of work as stockbrokers are dealing with vast sums of other people's money. Stockbrokers must be registered with the Financial Services Authority.

5 The Civil Service, local government and administration

The Civil Service

The Civil Service is one of the country's largest employers, providing work for nearly half a million people. It is made up of over 170 departments and agencies. It is the role of the departments to work with the government to formulate policies, while the agencies deliver them. The belief that civil servants wear bowler hats and work in stuffy offices in Whitehall is completely wrong, as is the idea that only graduates from Oxford and Cambridge are selected. The Civil Service stresses that it is looking for quality recruits from every walk of life. Legal graduates are often particularly well suited to a career in the Civil Service.

Only one in five posts is in London and the range of opportunity within the Civil Service is vast. Here are just some of its departments and agencies:

Cabinet Office
Central Science Laboratory
Centre for the Environment, Fisheries and Aquaculture Science
Charity Commission
Child Support Agency
Criminal Records Bureau
Crown Prosecution Service
Department for Culture, Media and Sport
Department for Education and Skills
Department for Environment, Food and Rural Affairs
Department for International Development
Department for Transport, Local Government and the Regions
Department of Health
Department of Trade and Industry
Food Standards Agency
Foreign and Commonwealth Office
Forensic Science Service
Forestry Commission
Historic Scotland
HM Customs and Excise

HM Immigration Service
HM Land Registry
HM Prison Service
HM Treasury
Home Office
Lord Chancellor's
  Department
Meteorological Office
Ministry of Defence
National Archives of Scotland
National Assembly for Wales
Northern Ireland Office
Office for Standards in
  Education (OFSTED)

Ordnance Survey
Patent Office
Public Record Office
Royal Parks Agency
Serious Fraud Office
The Maritime and
  Coastguard Agency
The Passports and Records
  Agency
The Scottish Executive
Veterinary Medicines
  Directorate
Youth Justice Board

Departments and agencies recruit individually. Vacancies are advertised on the Civil Service website, in the press and in professional journals. Applicants must reply to a particular job advertisement. Departments and agencies do not hold details on file to consider when a suitable vacancy arises.

The Fast Stream

This is the Civil Service accelerated development programme. By no means all graduates join by this route, but those who do are guaranteed a series of intensive job placements designed to prepare them for senior management positions. They move regularly between projects, take up postings in different departments and agencies and are seconded to Europe and the USA.

To apply for the Fast Stream you must be a UK national with at least an upper second class degree in any subject.

The General Fast Stream has five options:

★ Central Departments
★ Science and Engineering

What can I do with... a law degree?

★ European Fast Stream
★ Diplomatic Service
★ Clerkships in Parliament.

In addition there are specialist fast streams: Statisticians, Economists and Government Communications Headquarters.

The starting salary for Fast Streamers in London is around £19,000, going up to £34,000 on promotion and rising eventually to around £48,000.

Opportunities in Europe

European Fast Stream is designed to increase the number of British graduates securing permanent posts in EU institutions, It offers four years of training and work experience intended to improve chances of success in EU recruitment competitions. No particular language qualifications are required as these are developed during training. A small number of qualified lawyers are recruited under the scheme while in the UK they are attached to the Government Legal Service.

The European Commission holds regular competitions for recruitment to its administrative grades. All graduates may apply but a legal background is seen as particularly useful. It isn't possible to qualify as a lawyer within the Commission but in some cases a stage or programme of five months' work can count towards a training contract or pupillage.

Skills

Rather than looking for graduates with particular qualifications, the Civil Service aims to find young people from wide-ranging academic backgrounds who possess what it calls 'core competencies'.

These are:

★ the ability to challenge and think beyond conventional ideas
★ decisiveness – leadership ability
★ lucidity – expressing complicated ideas simply
★ robustness – coping well under pressure
★ a collaborative attitude – working as part of a team
★ an inquisitive mind – a questioning approach
★ adaptability – dealing with the unexpected
★ impartiality – not allowing your personal views to affect your work
★ sensitivity – being aware of the effect your decisions could have on others.

The majority of these skills, the ability to challenge and question, to make decisions and accept responsibility for them, to argue logically and to work as part of a team are exactly the qualities that have been identified as the ones likely to be developed during studies for a law degree.

Elissavet Kapnopoulou
Member of the Legal Service, European Court of Auditors

Degree: First degree in Law, Master's degree in Economic and Commercial Law
Thessaloniki University, Greece
PhD, University of Saarland, Germany

Elissavet works as part of the legal team that deals with legal problems arising out of the audit work of the European Court of Auditors. This European institution examines the revenue and expenditure of the European Union, making sure that money collected from European taxpayers is obtained and spent in a lawful and regular way.

Based in Luxembourg, she deals with cases that have been referred to the Legal Service for examination. Her working languages are French and English. Elissavet speaks seven languages, including her native Greek and international sign language.

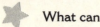

In her words, 'The great thing about working in a foreign country is that you rise above your own limits and discover things about yourself you would never find out if you stayed at home. For instance I know that it's difficult at first working in a foreign language, but I can do it.'

Elissavet's first posting with the EU was to Alicante in Spain, where she learned Spanish, and she is soon to take up a new post with the Council of the European Union in Brussels, which will include legal work and the management of human resources.

Describing herself as 'talkative', Elissavet feels: 'The most enjoyable aspect of my legal studies was the opportunity to study different legal systems and to debate and challenge ideas with others.'

Her determination to develop her language skills stems from Elissavet's belief that 'Law is the way forward to a peaceful future.'

Hans Moch
Patent Agent

A-levels: botany, zoology, chemistry
Degree: BSc Botany, Manchester University
BA Law, Manchester Metropolitan University

A patent is a kind of contract between the Crown and an inventor. In exchange for a full disclosure of the invention and provided that the invention is new, non-obvious and capable of industrial application, the inventor is given a 20-year monopoly on his or her invention to prevent anybody else from copying it. This is the way in which an industrialised society encourages the commercial investment required to make and exploit new inventions.

Patent agents stand between the Patent Office, which grants the patent, and the inventor. Their job is to draft the patent specification, which is the detailed description of the invention, accompanied by the claims, which are the legal definitions of the invention in terms that enable competitors to decide whether or not they infringe the patent.

When patent disputes arise the patent agent is assisted by a patent solicitor and a patent barrister who will usually have more conventional legal backgrounds.

Patent law is part of what is generally known as Intellectual Property Law, which includes trade marks, industrial designs and copyright. Patent agents work in firms that have specialists in all these areas. Today a firm is likely to have law graduate entry into the trade mark side of the work.

A patent agent's client will usually be a company or perhaps a university but sometimes individuals working on their own come up with good ideas that they want to protect. Hans did a lot of work for a large German company making cigarette-manufacturing equipment and also for a local company making speciality papers such as the ones used in tea bags.

After passing his professional examinations to become a chartered patent agent or patent attorney, and working for several years as a qualified attorney, Hans decided to study for a law degree by taking evening classes twice a week for four years.

He explains, 'I was fascinated with the law of patents, trade marks and designs and wanted to broaden my horizons and put this knowledge in a wider context of general law.

'As well as helping me in my work, I found that the general law I was studying made sense of ordinary life. For example, contract law reveals the network of legal relationships that lies just under the surface of daily life. So when you board a bus and buy a ticket you enter into a contract with obligations on both sides: the bus company undertakes to take you from A to B safely and on time; you agree to behave properly and pay the fare.

'I knew that if I made hard work of my course I wouldn't complete it so I decided to treat it as a hobby. For the same reason when I had to do a project I chose something that interested me and was important in my job: the law of spare parts.'

Local government

Local authorities such as county councils, borough councils and district councils provide a range of services to the community including education, finance, housing, libraries and social services. In order to do this they employ over two and a half million people.

Departments within local authorities employ administrators to plan and organise activities and to set up the systems needed to put in place the decisions passed by elected councillors. They manage staff, prepare the paperwork required by committees, process statistics, write reports and often deal with finance. Openings in local government are advertised in the local and sometimes the national press.

The skills needed for local government work correspond closely to those required by the Civil Service and fit closely with those gained through legal studies.

Rachel Nixon, having worked in both England and Northern Ireland, found a job that exactly fitted her academic qualifications and her work experience, literally within a few miles of her home, working for her local borough council!

Rachel Nixon
Executive Officer, Ards Borough Council, Northern Ireland

A-levels: French, German, economics
Degree: LLB European Law with Languages, University of the West of England
Legal Practice Course, Nottingham Law School

'I've absolutely no regrets about taking a degree in law. It was the best subject I could have chosen.'

Today Rachel Nixon is Executive Officer to the Ards Borough Council in Northern Ireland. Her role is to support the town clerk and chief executive, carrying out research, preparing material for meetings, writing reports, studying and advising on the impact of proposed or actual legislation or other government policies on the council.

The job outline specified a background in law and when she applied Rachel had a law degree plus several years' management experience with Sainsbury's.

Rachel recalls: 'We were the first students to take the European Law with Languages course and it was both exciting and demanding. It lasted four years, with one year spent working abroad. I spent the time in Germany working for six months in Mainz in the legal department of a bank and the rest in Wiesbaden in a solicitor's office.

'When I completed my degree I took the one-year full-time Legal Practice Course in Nottingham. My original plan was to complete my legal training in England and then return home to Northern Ireland. However I found it difficult to find articled work with a solicitor in England and decided to return to Northern Ireland.

'There the training system is different and involves gaining a place at the Institute of Professional Legal Studies. Competition is extremely tough and I tried two years running to gain a place without success.

'Money was becoming a problem. Although I had a job in a solicitor's office I began to feel I needed to rethink my career. I started temping and ended up in a bank working in administration and IT. I then applied successfully for a place as a retail graduate trainee with Sainsbury's.

'I was based in Belfast but spent my first year in Stoke-on-Trent, before being posted back to the Forestside store in Belfast. Within six months I was grocery manager at the Craigavon store in County Armagh, managing and training staff, making sure the shop floor was filled with goods and taking my turn as night duty manager.

'I then joined Sainsbury's retail systems team, introducing new IT systems into stores. I was living in Northern Ireland and working both there and in stores in the North of England. Gradually the amount of time I was spending in England increased and I found myself away from home more often than I was there.

'When I saw my present job advertised it seemed to offer everything I wanted – responsibility, challenge, opportunities and the chance to live at home.

'I'm very glad I studied law. I couldn't do my present job without the theoretical and practical experience I gained. I think it's important for students to realise there's far more to a legal career than being a solicitor or a barrister.'

Andy Piper
Head of Environmental Protection, King's Lynn, and West Norfolk Borough Council

A-levels: English literature, geography
Degree: LLB, London University

Andy's job involves dealing with hygiene and health and safety issues, inspecting houses and food premises and responding to complaints, for example of noise or unpleasant smells.

He opted to take a law degree in his spare time while working full time and found it not only stimulating but also helpful in his work.

'My work in environmental health introduced me to certain aspects of the law such as land law, administration law and rules of evidence. I would look at cases as part of my job and found myself becoming fascinated by the subject itself.

'The course took five years to complete because I took a year off when I changed my job. It involved a great deal of home study, which meant I had to discipline myself to go upstairs and shut the door even when the sun was shining and everyone else was outside.

'I really enjoyed it, but it was immensely hard work with quite a number of "semi-crisis moments" when I came close to being overwhelmed with the amount I had to do.'

Although Andy began his studies because he wanted intellectual stimulation, he did at one time consider taking up a legal career.

'A local solicitor heard about my studies and offered me a training position with his firm. I was tempted but my career in environmental health was taking off at that time and I decided to stay with it.'

However his degree in law has definitely been of benefit to Andy. 'Gaining a degree in law certainly boosted my self esteem. It's highly regarded by people and through my studies I now have a wider understanding of law as it relates to my work. It's a bit like owning a car. You don't have to know how it works in order to drive it, but it's helpful if you do.'

Administration

The term 'chartered secretary' is unfortunate as it suggests providing clerical support to people who make the decisions. Nothing could be further from the truth. Private and public companies are required by law to appoint a company secretary and many large organisations have company secretarial departments.

Chartered secretaries are employed as company secretaries and administrators in business, commerce, education, charities, investment trusts, hospitals and local authorities. The professional body, the Institute of Chartered Secretaries and Administrators (ICSA), has found this area of work attracts many law graduates. A career as a chartered secretary requires many of the transferable skills gained during legal studies and provides an opportunity to use legal knowledge while working in a wider environment.

A recent survey conducted by ICSA found that the majority of company secretaries earn between £65,000 and £80,000 a year, with 20 per cent earning over £110,000.

The job

The work of a chartered secretary includes:

★ ensuring an organisation complies with business law
★ communicating with shareholders

★ organising annual general meetings
★ having overall responsibility for pensions, employee share schemes, insurance, health and safety and personnel.

Company secretaries working in smaller organisations tend to have a wider role than those with large companies. Over 20 per cent of ICSA members who responded to a 2000–1 survey worked at director or board level.

Getting in

Graduates are exempt from the first part of the ICSA qualifying examinations. They have to complete the bridging programme modules covering financial accounting, corporate law, strategic and operations management and management accounting, plus the professional programme modules of corporate governance, corporate secretaryship, corporate administration and corporate financial management. Study is usually on a part-time basis while working in a relevant job. Around 70 per cent of trainees have their fees paid by their employers. After three years' relevant work graduates can apply for associate membership and for fellowship after five years.

The best way to find a job is to contact a specialist recruitment agency such as ICSA Consultants (see Chapter 15 – Useful addresses) and to check for advertisements in the *Chartered Secretary* magazine. Some job seekers start the training and then look for work as a part-qualified ICSA student as there are more openings for part-qualified trainees than for those embarking on the training. Salaries for part-qualified trainees are around £27,000.

Emma Turner
Company Secretarial Assistant, Hilton Group plc

Degree: LLB, De Montfort University

Emma found out by chance about a career as a company secretary.

She explains, 'I was actually working at the Further Education Funding Council, where I used to inspect colleges, and I came across the information on ICSA (the professional body for company secretaries) there.

'After graduating I knew I wanted to use my skills in law, but I wanted something more business oriented than being a solicitor. Becoming a company secretary at the Hilton Group was ideal. By working at the head office I've gained vital skills in all areas of company secretarial work, including plenty of overseas statutory matters.

'Hilton Group has about 500 subsidiary companies and two divisions, hotels and betting and gaming, for which I help maintain the records and prepare minutes throughout the year as the need arises. I also help out at the company's annual general meeting. My work is always varied. No two days are ever the same.

'I started studying for the ICSA qualifying exams straight away and was able to use that knowledge in my day-to-day work. I'm lucky because the company pays for my study package and gives me days off to revise for exams. The working and the studying are quite hard going, but I think the qualification is a very good one because it covers management skills as well as accounting.

'My law degree has given me an advantage, particularly in company and contract law. When I first started in this job I already understood a lot of the terminology. Work experience placements had given me the confidence and ability to deal with people at all levels, from individual shareholders to senior managers. Studying law also gives you a sense of judgement so I can always see the legal implications of my work.'

6 Personnel or human resources

The terms 'personnel' and 'human resources' are often interchangeable, although the term 'personnel' tends to refer to the day-to-day issues concerned with employee relations, while 'human resources' covers longer-term strategic aspects.

The work involves recruiting the best people for the job and training and managing them to meet their full potential, thus making the organisation that employs them as efficient as possible.

Openings in personnel are to be found in a wide range of organisations, including department stores, supermarkets and factories, banks, health services, airlines, hotels, further and higher education institutes and travel companies. Whatever the setting, the work includes dealing with tricky issues such as disputes and disciplinary matters.

Personnel staff often find themselves entrusted with confidential information. They need to balance the best interests of the individual against what is best for the organisation and have to be prepared to carry out unpleasant tasks such as dealing with redundancies, grievance procedures and dismissals.

This is why personnel professionals need the following qualities:

★ a fair and objective attitude
★ a firm, calm approach to every situation
★ diplomatic skills
★ an approachable manner
★ good interpersonal skills
★ good communication skills
★ ability to cope confidently with statistics.

A number of these skills, such as interpersonal and communication skills, and a calm objective approach to the work, are among the skills gained from a law degree.

Starting salaries are in the range of £15,000–£17,000, while salaries for personnel directors can go beyond £60,000.

The job

The work carried out in personnel departments varies according to the organisation, its size and its workforce.

In large departments personnel professionals may specialise in a particular area such as employee relations, whereas in smaller organisations they tend to be generalists. Personnel departments work closely with other departments within an organisation.

The main areas of work are:

★ **Recruitment and selection**
  – drawing up job descriptions
  – preparing advertisements
  – checking applications forms
  – carrying out interviews
  – selecting new staff
  – obtaining references.
★ **Employee development**
  – drawing up training programmes, using internal staff or specialist training organisations
  – running induction courses for newcomers
  – carrying out regular appraisals for personnel, helping them to build on their strengths and improve their weak areas.
★ **Employee relations**
  – handling differences between staff members
  – negotiating with trade unions on pay and working conditions

- dealing with grievances, disciplinary proceedings
- implementing redundancy programmes.

★ **Employee services**
- dealing with health and safety matters and community relations issues
- keeping staff records
- having responsibility for medical, sports and social facilities.

★ **Reward**
- evaluating jobs
- administering benefits and payroll systems.

★ **Human resource planning**
- predicting future staffing levels and the skills that will be needed to deal with possible changes.

Getting in

The Chartered Institute of Personnel and Development (CIPD) considers law, together with degree subjects such as psychology and business studies, to be particularly suited to personnel work.

The professional qualification is the CIPD Professional Development Scheme. This involves around two years' part-time study. Most people opt to study for the PDS while working in a personnel-type job. However it is possible to study for the qualification on a full-time basis. Another option is to study for a Master's level qualification. Many universities and colleges run human resources programmes leading to a diploma or postgraduate degree. If these have been approved by the CIPD they can lead automatically to graduate membership.

Non-approved postgraduate courses are assessed by the CIPD and can lead to exemption from part of the professional examinations.

There is strong competition for personnel jobs and no matter how well qualified you may be you are unlikely to find work without relevant practical experience. This could be a holiday job in a personnel department, work experience or responsibilities held at university organising a society, sports club or fund raising event.

A degree in law is likely to be an asset in personnel work, not only because of the background knowledge of employment law it provides but also for the soft or transferable skills gained from the course.

Personnel posts are advertised in the national press, careers websites and in professional journals such as *People Management*.

7 Library and information management

The old idea of librarians spending their time buried silently behind piles of books couldn't be further from the truth. Today librarians not only work with books but with videos, audio-cassettes, CDs, computer systems and the Internet. For this reason they are becoming known as information managers, specialists or professionals.

Graduates with law degrees plus a librarian/information management qualification are in a good position to find work in a legal firm, in the same way that graduates with qualifications in science, the arts, or music are in demand in specialist libraries.

Information managers need:

★ advanced IT skills
★ wide knowledge of the Internet
★ an outgoing and approachable manner
★ good communication skills
★ an organised, logical and methodical approach to work.

Communication skills and the methodical approach to work are among the transferable skills gained through legal degree courses.

Starting salaries for information managers range from £15,000–£17,000 in the London area, slightly less in other parts of the country.

The job

Information managers not only work in public or academic libraries, but in legal firms, medical organisations, scientific establishments, finance, industry, commerce, the media and wherever people need to access information.

Their role is to manage information. They find material that has been requested and they advise enquirers on how to access information for themselves using websites and online databases as well as books and journals. They carry out research, analyse information, extract relevant sections, store and retrieve material. Information managers also create new information systems to meet the specific needs of their organisations.

Getting in

The Standing Conference of National and University Libraries (SCONUL) scheme enables graduates who are looking for a career in library and information management to spend a trainee year working in related employment in order to gain supervised experience of the work. Employers involved in the scheme undertake to provide trainees with an overall view of the library system and experience of the day-to-day operation of a library.

After completing the trainee year students can go on to a full-time course or apply for a job, and either study part time for a professional qualification or delay further study for a while.

Certain charities offer voluntary work opportunities in library and information management. Details of these and the SCONUL scheme are available from the Chartered Institute of Library and Information Professionals (CILIP) (see Chapter 15 – Useful addresses).

The CILIP is the professional body for librarians and information managers or specialists. There are two levels of membership: Membership (MCLIP) and Fellowship (FCLIP).

Candidates can apply for associateship if they have a degree or diploma recognised by the CILIP. Applicants need either to submit a report or portfolio showing how their technical knowledge has been applied in their job or to complete an application form and undergo an interview. Most applicants gain membership after two or three years in work.

There are specialist recruitment agencies for library and information management work. CILIP runs its own, called Infomatch, and there are several others.

Gail Sanderson
Director of Information Services, Davies Arnold Cooper

A-levels: English, French, history
Degree: LLB, Brunel University

Gail works in a city legal firm with more than 40 partners, specialising in commercial litigation and property law. She heads a team of five full-time information service staff, all of them with first or second degrees in information management and two with law degrees.

The work of the team includes creating, running and maintaining the firm's Intranet system, producing daily electronic bulletins covering any legal changes and a weekly, paper bulletin.

The team evaluates online legal services to decide whether they would be of value to the firm as research tools and provides training in legal research for trainee solicitors, who in Gail's view, 'know a lot about the law and very little about legal information'. Legal staff also put in requests for legal research to be carried out by Gail and her team, which also accesses business and commercial information for the firm.

Gail prefers the term 'information manager' to librarian because, as she says, 'Only a small amount of our work is with books. Our main focus is the delivery of electronic information both proactively and reactively.'

Her interest in law developed during her first job in a consumer advice centre in which she was involved with contract law and consumer rights. She went on to take a law degree at Brunel University that included three work placements.

As a result of these periods spent in legal practices Gail began to realise that it was law in the abstract that fascinated her, rather than its practical application. She took a part-time postgraduate librarian course while her children were young, although in her words, 'I was never interested in working in a public library, only in a legal environment'.

Gail's decision to look for work with a legal firm came at a good time. 'Previously, research work tended to be put out to barristers, but legal firms were just beginning to realise this was expensive and that it might be more cost effective and efficient to employ somebody in the firm to do the work.'

She began working two days a week and as the firm quadrupled in size within eight years, so the demand for the services of her team grew.

Today there are moves in many firms to digitilise archives and practice documents such as precedents. As an increasing amount of material is stored electronically there is a growing need for legal taxonomies or the creation of an artificial index so that material can be stored and retrieved without problems.

Knowledge management has become an important area of activity for larger law firms and as Gail points out, the role of the information manager along with the entire area of work is set to grow significantly in the future. It is also one to which the skills and knowledge of the law graduate are particularly well suited.

8   Information technology

Just 40 years ago there were six computers in the world. Today over 72 million computers all over the globe are linked by the Internet, despite the fact that ten years ago nobody had heard of the World Wide Web.

Almost all organisations rely on information technology (IT) in some way: to increase efficiency, to cut down costs or to provide a better service. More than one million people work as IT professionals in the UK, 45 per cent in the IT industry itself and 55 per cent in other industries. The industry is expanding and requires between 150,000 and 200,000 additional professionals every year. Around half of the graduates recruited to work in the IT industry do not have IT degrees.

Many employers are looking for particular qualities rather than technical qualifications. These include:

★ problem-solving abilities
★ strong communication skills
★ the ability to work as part of a team.

These are some of the major skills gained from legal studies, so it is not surprising that law graduates fit well into the world of IT.

The use of psychometric tests as part of the selection process is becoming more widespread because they give employers an idea of a candidate's ability to pick up new skills. Links to sites containing examples of such tests can be found on the e-skills website. (See Chapter 15 – Useful addresses.)

Starting salaries for graduates going into IT vary greatly according to the size and geographical location of a company. They are often high – over £19,000 is not unusual.

The jobs

Job opportunities in IT can be roughly divided into four groups:

★ Operations
★ Services
★ Sales and marketing
★ Research and development.

Operations

Most large organisations run their own IT systems supported by their specialist IT operations department, which ensures the efficient running of the systems, introduces upgrades when necessary and decides on future developments to meet the changing needs of the company.

Job opportunities include:

★ Systems analyst
★ Network manager
★ Database administrator.

Services

Companies that do not have specialist IT departments buy in services as required. IT service companies offer a range of services and job opportunities including:

★ IT consultant
★ Project manager
★ Technical architect
★ Hardware engineer.

Sales and marketing

Systems and software packages are constantly being upgraded, and personnel with technical and sales skills are needed to visit clients, introduce new products and services and talk over their requirements.

Jobs include:

★ Client manager
★ Technical sales specialist
★ Marketing professional.

Research and development

The challenge to develop new products is enormous and work linked to this includes testing, correcting problems and writing user manuals.

Job opportunities include:

★ Software developer
★ Technical author.

Getting in

Employers need graduates to become a useful part of the business as soon as possible.

In response to this the e-skills Graduate Apprenticeship programme has been drawn up by the e-skills training organisation together with employers and educators across the country. It provides the first stage of a structured professional development path for IT professionals at entry level and has three key elements:

★ an honours degree
★ key skills certificates
★ technical/optional units certificates selected to reflect the student's area of work.

External training courses
While many employers seek out non-IT graduates with the right qualities and train them from scratch, some graduates opt for some form of IT training before looking for work.

However, if you are thinking of investing time and money in a training course, make sure the training on offer is right for you, that it is relevant to the type of job you want and that the qualification itself is valued by employers.

Short courses
These are offered by FE colleges and private companies as well as universities and can also be studied online. Some employers still want relevant work experience from candidates with these qualifications, but they are a way into the industry.

Options include:

★ IT user qualifications such as RSA and the European Computer Driving Licence
★ Vendor qualifications such as Microsoft and Cisco
★ Programming languages such as Visual basic and HTML.

Postgraduate IT conversion courses
These courses usually last one year full time, although many are offered on a part-time basis or as evening study. The content varies but is likely to cover such subjects as software and hardware, analysis and design, databases and programming. The increasing demand for web-related skills and e-commerce has led to an increase in such courses. Entry requirements are usually a first degree plus evidence of an interest in IT and for some courses relevant work experience. The average cost of a course is around £3000.

Contacts
With over one million people working in IT, everybody knows somebody working in the industry and such contacts are a good starting point in finding out what the industry has to

offer. If you're interested in a career in IT you will need to do plenty of research, reading up on IT job descriptions and comparing them with your own skills and interests to gain an idea of the sort of work that would suit you.

IT employers complain that students make little use of contacts and suggest as starting points talking to IT personnel at careers fairs, contacting companies where you have previously done work experience, even if it was not in IT, and discussing your plans with friends and family, lecturers and university staff.

Work experience is vital when considering any type of job and research shows that a high percentage of people who start with a work placement in IT are offered employment. If a work placement isn't possible, temporary work in almost any business can be a stepping stone.

IT vacancies are to be found on websites and a good place to start is the e-skills employer list on the e-skills website. *The Daily Telegraph*, *The Financial Times*, *The Times* and *The Guardian* all have IT sections in their job vacancies sections.

Jennifer Trayner
Executive, Global Risk Management Solutions, PriceWaterhouseCoopers

Scottish Highers: English, history, Latin, classical studies, drama, biology, economics
Degree: LLB, University of Aberdeen

It was during the third year of a four-year degree course that Jennifer began to question whether she wanted a legal career.

'I was filling in application forms for legal traineeships and when I came to the question "Why do you want to be a solicitor?" I couldn't think of an answer. I'd had work experience with a criminal lawyer when I was 16 and had enjoyed it, especially going to court, but when I thought about it I had no really good reason to be a solicitor. The time had come to think about alternative careers.'

Jennifer knew she was interested in business and after graduation took temporary jobs for a few months while investigating opportunities, surfing the Web for openings with financial institutions. She wasn't interested in accountancy, but felt there must be other openings, and when she saw her present job advertised immediately e-mailed her application. Within a week she was in Birmingham on an induction course.

She explains, 'There are two sides to my job. One is examining all the processes involved in a client's business. For example if a client is offering pensions, I check the process from the initial application form to the final pension agreement. The second part of my work is making sure the IT systems used are secure, that they are adequately maintained and the processes are correct. What I am interested in is how the business processes and IT systems generate the financial figures and how the business ensures these are accurate.'

Since joining the company Jennifer has trained in a number of IT operating systems including Mainframe Security, Windows NT and Unix. Her job involves long hours of work, to which she is accustomed, thanks to her degree. Her studies, she feels, 'made me able to cope with a challenge, work long hours and understand the legal aspects of business'.

IT is a growing area of employment and one that makes use of many of the skills possessed by legal graduates.

9 Journalism and publishing

Journalism

More than 130 daily and Sunday newspapers are published in the UK, plus 800 weeklies, 1000 local free newspapers, 2000 consumer magazines and 4500 business and professional publications. The total number of magazines on the shelves has grown by over 30 per cent in the last ten years and the same period has seen rapid expansion in satellite broadcasting.

This means good opportunities for the right type of person, although entry into journalism is a competitive business and the work is not for the faint hearted, or for those who like regular hours and plenty of free time.

Qualities needed for a career in journalism are:

★ an inquisitive interest in everything
★ highly developed communication skills
★ a good knowledge of the rules of punctuation and grammar
★ an approachable manner
★ good IT skills
★ self-confidence to face criticism and deal with difficult situations
★ ability to work as part of a team
★ good self-management skills.
★ attention to detail
★ enthusiasm and energy.

Of these, self-confidence, strong communication skills, teamwork, attention to detail and self-management are the skills mentioned by many of the profile subjects as the strengths they gained through their studies.

Salaries for trainee journalists vary from paper to paper, but are usually in the region of £12,000-£14,000.

The job

Journalism can be divided into the following categories, although journalists often move from one medium to another:

★ newspaper journalism
★ magazine journalism
★ broadcast journalism – national and local radio stations and television companies
★ news media agency journalism – supplying stories to newspapers and magazines
★ public relations – working in the PR department or press office of an organisation, trying to ensure it receives positive press coverage.

Getting in

Graduates with degrees in any subject can make a career in journalism. Success lies more in having the right skills than in possessing particular academic qualifications.

Whatever route you take into journalism you will need evidence of your skills and enthusiasm in the form of articles published in student newspapers, freelance articles in local free or paid newspapers or involvement in community, campus or hospital radio stations.

Of new entrants to journalism 70–80 per cent have taken a postgraduate course in journalism. Full-time courses recognised by the National Council for the Training of Journalists (NCTJ) or the Broadcast Journalism Training Council (BJTC) in various aspects of journalism are available at colleges in the UK and Northern Ireland. Part-time courses are also available. There are still some opportunities for graduates to be recruited directly into jobs as journalism trainees on magazines and newspapers and as broadcast trainees by television companies.

Camilla Tominey
Trainee Reporter, *Hemel Hempstead Gazette*

A-levels: English literature, French, history
Degree: LLB, Leeds University

'By the end of my time at university I knew the last thing I wanted to be was a lawyer. Looking back I wanted to study law, but I was never certain I wanted to be a lawyer. During my second year I did work experience with two massive legal firms in London and felt very out of place. I nicknamed them "giggle-free zones" and knew they weren't for me.'

After graduation Camilla spent almost a year travelling in Asia and Australia. On her return she took a job in a pub to keep the cash flowing and started to think seriously about the future.

'I liked the idea of journalism and wrote to a number of newspapers asking about jobs and training. The editor of the *Hemel Hempstead Gazette*, who had recently been let down by a trainee, invited me for an interview and offered me a job.

'The *Gazette* is a weekly paid-for newspaper with a free newspaper attached to it. The atmosphere in the office is completely different from that of the legal firms and I liked it instantly.

'I've been with the *Gazette* for two years and I'm soon to finish my training and take my National Certificate Exam, to qualify as a senior journalist capable of reporting on anything. As part of my training I spent three months on a residential course in Sheffield and I've built up a portfolio demonstrating the range of work I've done.

'As part of my job I'm the district reporter for Berkhamsted. The hours are long and include evenings covering events such as council meetings. I also take photographs when necessary. The pay is low compared with the law, but that doesn't matter

to me because I love the job. It's never boring and a
qualification in journalism can open a lot of doors – work on
national newspapers, magazines, radio, television.

'Do I regret my time studying law? Not at all. I enjoyed my time
at university and knowledge of the law is vital for a journalist,
so a lot of what I learned is a help to me in my job.'

Caroline Lashley is Press Officer with the Probation Training
Unit. She gained her law degree by studying part time while at
work, but decided to stay in public relations rather than follow
a legal career.

Caroline Lashley
Press Officer, Probation Training Unit

HND Business Studies
Degree: LLB, Westminster University

As Press Officer for the Probation Training Unit Caroline
spends her days answering the phone and dealing with press
enquiries. She also organises visits for overseas guests eager to
see how the probation service operates in the UK. This includes
arranging for them to see courts, hostels, community service
units and programme centres and to meet probation officers
and talk to them about their work.

Caroline studied for her law degree part time while working at
the Probation Training Unit and has never regretted it, although
she admits it was hard work at the time. One reason why she
found law an attractive choice was that it is seen as a serious
option and one that involves a great deal of work.

She says, 'Coming from a working-class, ethnic background, my
family saw education as very important. A law degree was the
ultimate achievement and since I've graduated I feel my
confidence has grown. I'm not afraid to state an opinion and I
know my views are worth listening to.'

Much as she enjoyed her studies Caroline decided not to
continue with professional training after her degree.

'I remember talking to someone who mentioned it would take me a further five years after my degree to become a barrister. My reaction was that I wanted my life back. I'd put it on hold for quite a long time, studying, working, not going out, never having any money.

'When I was younger I'd taken a radio journalism course and during my law course I'd chosen optional courses in entertainment law and family law, which fitted in well with my present job.

'For me the achievement of a law degree was tremendous and the skills and knowledge I gained will always be there.'

Publishing

Work in publishing depends a great deal on the type of material being produced – newspapers, books or magazines. Newspaper and magazine editors usually have a journalism background.

The job

Commissioning editors research the market to find out what people want to read, then decide on new titles. They commission authors to write the work, brief them on exactly what is required, keep in touch during writing to iron out any difficulties, check and amend completed copy and decide on the layout and final appearance of the publication.

Publishing companies receive unsolicited work from authors who send it in the hope that it will be accepted. While the vast majority of such manuscripts are returned, some great literary success stories have begun life as unsolicited manuscripts and no publisher can afford to miss the chance of a best seller. Commissioning editors organise readers to deal with the huge pile of unsolicited material, and to pass back the ones that merit a closer look.

Editors need the following qualities:

★ good organisational skills
★ strong technical writing skills with a high level of accuracy in spelling and punctuation
★ an up-to-date knowledge of literary trends – what types of books are being read
★ the ability to analyse sales material
★ a good business eye
★ the ability to work with and motivate other people.

All of these are important but, given the role of an editor as the central point in the book production process, strong organisational skills are vital and these are gained from studying law.

Getting in

The way into a career in publishing is often through a job as an editorial assistant with a publishing company. Editorial assistants do whatever is required: photocopying, researching possible new areas of interest for publications, making contact with authors, drawing up agreements and proof-reading material. This way they gain the experience they need to apply for a more senior post, such as commissioning editor.

There are postgraduate courses in publishing available at a number of universities and the Publishing Training Centre has a list of these (see Chapter 15 – Useful addresses). However the majority of graduates with degrees in all subjects get into publishing by taking whatever job they can.

Employers are looking for practical knowledge of publishing, either through work experience, holiday jobs or involvement in college or university publications. A knowledge of proof-reading could be helpful. This demands an eye for detail and knowledge of the correction symbols used in the process. These can be self-taught with the aid of a book such as *The*

What can I do with... a law degree?

Writers' and Artists' Year Book or studied through a correspondence course.

Jobs advertised in the national press attract hundreds of replies and smaller companies often advertise in the specialist press such as *Press Gazette*, *Media Week*, *The Bookseller* and *Publishing News.*

Homework and research are essential – visiting book fairs, making contacts with people in publishing and finding out about openings, often with small, specialist publishers.

Stephanie Russon
Publisher

A-levels: English literature, geography, biology, general studies
Degree: LLB, Manchester Metropolitan University

Stephanie is a publisher with a personal finance and education publishing company. She explains: 'Our average reader is 40-plus years old, with money to invest. One of the most important parts of my job is to come up with hot topics to interest readers. For example at the moment a major concern is the unsettled state of the stock market, which means readers are looking for secure ways of investing their money.

'Once I've decided on a topic I research it to see what material is already available, before commissioning a new piece to be written. Then I organise a marketing campaign, which can take the form of direct mailings, inserts, books and courses. If an idea doesn't work, I take the blame.'

Despite the high level of responsibility she has in the company, Stephanie began her work there as a temp only four years ago.

She says, 'My original intention when I started my degree course was to train as a solicitor, but by the time I had finished I was worried about the cost of training on top of the expenses I had already accumulated. Added to this was the knowledge that not all trainees can find a training contract with a qualified solicitor to complete the last part of their training.

'While I worked out exactly what I wanted to do I went home to the Midlands and did temporary work for four months. Then I moved to London and started temping.

'My first job was with an accountancy firm and I hated it so much I registered with a second agency and was sitting doing their basic tests when the phone rang. It was my present company. They were desperate for a temp so the agency told me to stop doing the tests and get over there immediately!'

For the first few months Stephanie answered the phone, did the filing and made herself useful. When a permanent member of staff left she applied for the job and today she has her own department with five people working for her.

Despite not working in the legal profession, Stephanie has no regrets about taking a law degree and feels that it has helped her to cope with her present job.

'Studying law means you learn to think logically and speak out with confidence. You're always being questioned, so you never say anything that you can't back up. It helps you to recognise waffle and cut through it quickly.

'A lot of my work is carrying out research and a law course certainly prepared me for this. I also think having a law degree is an asset in the job market because employers are impressed by it. The downside of this is the fact that the course is very heavy and demanding. Nobody can ever say a law degree is an easy option!'

Does Stephanie regret not completing her professional studies and becoming a solicitor as she originally planned?

'I enjoy the work I do now and the idea of returning to study is not something I very often think about. You're only given a certain amount of time after gaining a degree to finish your professional training and I must be getting close to the limit. I have a mortgage, so giving up my job isn't a realistic option and I'm not sure I'd want to do it even if it were.'

Stephanie's profile shows how the skills she gained from her legal studies: communication skills, self-confidence, the ability to 'cut through the waffle' to the central point of an argument, are exactly the ones required in publishing.

10   Advertising and Marketing

Advertising

The advertising industry is massive, with over £13 billion being spent every year persuading people to buy food, drink, perfume, holidays, music, insurance, to support good causes and to live healthily.

Yet the advertising industry is vulnerable to change. When a company fears the onset of financial problems, advertising budgets are often the first to suffer, so advertising is one of the first areas to be hit by a recession. Most agencies in the UK are relatively small and tend to make staff redundant at the first hint of difficulty. Advertising can be an exciting world, well paid and lively, but it can also be precarious, with heavy pressure to meet deadlines and bring in clients.

Qualities needed to work in advertising are:

★ a lively, creative mind combined with a strong practical streak to turn ideas into reality
★ ability to work in a team
★ self-motivatation
★ self-confidence to cope with difficulties
★ plenty of energy, enthusiasm and determination
★ good interpersonal skills
★ good organisational skills.

As this list shows, the world of advertising requires in strong measure many of the skills gained from studying for a legal degree.

Starting salaries for graduates in advertising and marketing range from £12,000–16,000.

The jobs

The creative work of designing and realising the advertisements is usually carried out by staff with artistic training, but there are openings for graduates from other disciplines who have plenty of energy, confidence and strong interpersonal skills.

Account executives have direct contact with clients. They discuss their products, the size of their budgets and what they want from the advertising campaign. They then brief the agency staff on what is needed and act as the link between agency and client throughout the campaign. Most graduates come into advertising as account executives and those who are good at their job go on to become account directors.

Account planners analyse a client's requirements, carrying out market research and designing a detailed strategy to be used by the creative team. They also carry out research throughout the campaign to measure its success.

Media executives decide where the advertisements are to appear. They have to consider the amount of money available, the audiences the client needs to attract, the newspapers the target audience reads, the television programmes they watch, the places where they shop and eat and the routes they travel. Strong analytical skills are needed for this work.

Copywriters produce the words that form part of the advertisement and work closely with the artistic teams.

Getting in

Finding a job in advertising is not easy. One possible route is through media sales or selling advertising space. All publications rely on advertising to bring in the money that allows them to sell copies at a competitive price. Most media sales are carried out on the phone and the job requires tact and persuasion, plus a head for numbers, as customers are always asking for special rates and discounts.

There is no national training scheme for the advertising sector although the Communication, Advertising and Marketing (CAM) Education Foundation runs certificate and diploma qualifications and the Institute of Practitioners in Advertising runs training courses for advertising staff at all levels (see Chapter 15 – Useful addresses).

As you would expect in an area that is all about sales, selling yourself is the way in. In-depth research, eye-catching CVs, endless phone calls (both in response to job advertisements and on the off-chance that there might be a vacancy) are the ways in which people find work in advertising.

Antony Smith
Working in advertising

A-levels: English literature, history, classical civilisations
Degree: LLB English and European Law, Essex University

Acting on careers advice Antony did have work experience with a firm of solicitors. However it wasn't quite what he imagined. In his words, 'I spent almost all my time cleaning out the basement and left with very little idea of what went on upstairs.'

Remembering the advice of his careers teacher that there was a lot of money to be made in a legal career, Antony still went on to study English and European law at Essex University. He spent a year of the course in Copenhagen studying European contract law and human rights law, which he found very interesting and enjoyable.

After graduation his priority was to earn some money and he took a job selling advertising space, but soon realised this was not how he wanted to spend the rest of his working life. Antony applied for a European-funded legal training place in Brussels, but despite working hard he wasn't successful, because his language skills were not considered to be sufficiently strong.

Faced with completely rethinking his career and determined that he wasn't going to sell advertising again, Antony worked temporarily as a roofer. Although he hadn't enjoyed his selling job, it did help him to get his next job, creating ideas for advertising campaigns, and he soon found that he enjoyed thinking up advertising strategies for a wide range of publications including leisure magazines, TV guides and competition newsletters.

He has been in the job for three years and, while he thoroughly enjoys the work, he's glad he took a law degree.

In Antony's words, 'It was a great experience. I gained a lot from planning and giving presentations, especially the ones I did in Denmark. The course helped me to think and write logically and concisely and to argue my point. The discipline of the training has helped me to spot the central point of an argument very quickly and that's an asset in any job. I don't have any wish to become a lawyer, but I would enjoy a marketing job with a big legal firm.'

Marketing

The purpose of marketing is to provide customers with the goods or services they want to buy. This involves looking into current market trends to see what people are buying, how much they are spending, how they like goods to be packaged and presented.

It is the role of a marketing department to come up with new ideas for products, to test out sales opportunities and to work with other departments in an organisation to create a product or service that meets customer needs or tastes and so sells well.

To work in marketing you need to:

★ be creative, with ideas that are eye-catching and original
★ have the practical skills to turn these ideas into reality

★ analyse the position of your products against the competition
★ manage all aspects of a marketing campaign
★ work closely with other people including outside agencies
★ keep to a budget and a time scale
★ have strong financial skills to make sure that marketing activities lead to increased profit.

A strong spark of originality is clearly a vital ingredient for a career in marketing, but also essential are skills such as self-motivation, teamwork and powers of analysis, which are to be found to a high degree among legal graduates.

The jobs

Marketing can be divided into:

★ research and analysis – understanding markets
★ strategy and planning – developing strategies and marketing plans
★ brands – developing and managing brands and reputation
★ putting in place marketing programmes
★ managing products, services and customer relationships, setting prices, managing programmes and projects
★ managing effectiveness – monitoring and evaluating the effectiveness of the work
★ managing people.

Getting in

It is possible to find a job in marketing with a degree in any subject although an increasing number of graduates are choosing to take a full-time postgraduate course in marketing. Opportunities are available in many sectors, from food and drink manufacture to household goods such as washing machines and refrigerators, industrial machinery, insurance, travel and even schools and colleges.

Once in work, many employers encourage staff to study part time for a Chartered Institute of Marketing or Institute of Export qualification.

Marketing and advertising are exciting areas of work. They also demand a significant number of the skills gained from studying law.

There is strong competition for jobs in marketing and vacancies are advertised in professional publications such as *Marketing Week* and *Campaign*.

11   **Retail**

Asda, Debenhams, Tesco, Sainsbury's, John Lewis, Marks & Spencer – these are just a few of the retail stores offering high quality management training to graduates. There are literally dozens of companies trying to attract bright young people into their retail operations. Today retail has become such an important sector that it's possible to take a Master's degree in the subject.

Most management trainee programmes last between nine months and two years and combine working on the shop floor with block training in staff training centres. Programmes often involve one or two moves during the training period, so trainees do need to be flexible. A graduate who successfully completes a management trainee scheme can expect to be in a senior management position after three to five years.

Companies are more interested in the qualities of entrants than the subject of their degree. However many of the qualities they are looking for are similar to those gained through a law degree. These include:

★ confidence to work calmly under pressure
★ flexibility to adapt to changing situations
★ enthusiasm and willingness to work hard
★ good organisational and leadership skills
★ self-motivation and time management skills
★ strong communication skills
★ the ability to work as part of a team.

Salaries for trainees are between £12,000 and £18,000. The manager of a large supermarket or a sizeable retail operation on a prime site can earn between £50,000 and £60,000.

The jobs

Retail training opportunities fall into different categories.

Store manager

Managers are responsible for the day-to-day running of either a store or a department within a store, developing the business by increasing efficiency and customer satisfaction. They are responsible for staff, sales, customer service, stock control and the profitability of the store.

Typical work includes making management decisions on staff movement and stock control, analysing sales figures and predicting trends (usually with the use of IT), organising sales promotions, dealing with health and safety issues, carrying out staff appraisals and planning staff development programmes.

Retail buyer

Buyers are responsible for purchasing the goods to be sold in the store. They have to ensure the colours, designs and packaging of the goods fit the customers' tastes and spending patterns. Goods must also be priced competitively, to appeal to the customer and to give the store sufficient profit.

Work includes attending trade fairs and exhibitions to keep abreast of the latest developments, making contact with possible new sources of stock, meeting with wholesalers and negotiating terms. Once stock is in the store, buyers liaise closely with store managers and merchandisers, gauging customer reaction when making decisions, perhaps to reduce prices or to move stock into a different position on the sales floor. Buyers are also involved in the training of sales staff.

There are a few direct training schemes in buying, which tend to be in the fashion sector, but most buyers enter through general management training programmes and then move into buying.

Retail merchandiser

Merchandisers plan, organise and monitor the distribution of goods to retail outlets, making sure that products arrive at the right store on the right date and in the right quantity. Their role is vital because no matter how well-selected goods may be, if they are not on the shelves at the right time customers will buy elsewhere.

The job involves a great deal of numerical calculation and for this reason recruitment interviews may include psychometric testing of numerical ability. Merchandisers work extensively on computers and knowledge of spreadsheet packages and forecasting models is essential.

Once the buyers have selected a range the merchandisers start working with them, deciding the amount of stock to be purchased, forecasting sales and profits and planning promotions. Merchandisers negotiate with suppliers the details of the stock delivery programme. They visit production sites to ensure the manufacturing process is on schedule and up to standard. When problems arise in production and delivery, the merchandisers need to act quickly in order to minimise their effect on the store.

Further opportunities

In addition to retail training opportunities many stores offer management training in related areas such as human resources and finance. There are also openings for IT specialists, lawyers and other professionals in the head offices of retail operations.

Getting in

Most retail organisations have stands at careers fairs, websites containing careers information and booklets on management training opportunities. Recruitment programmes tend to run between October and May.

Previous retail experience is welcomed, which means those after-school and vacation jobs look good on a CV.

Peter Mayhew
Commercial Manager Store Operations, Marks & Spencer

Degree: LLB Law with Business, University of Hertfordshire

Peter describes himself as a latecomer to education: 'I left school at 16 with two GCSEs at Grade C. The following year I gained two more and went into work in general administration. I soon realised I was going to need qualifications for a decent job and took a BTEC in Business and Finance. I then gained an Association of Accounting Technicians qualification NVQ Level 4, which is equivalent to two to three A-levels, and I used it to apply to university to study law with business.'

Leaving university with an upper second class degree, Peter had a place waiting at the College of Law and planned to become a solicitor. Before starting the course he tried to find articles with a legal firm, but after writing 150 letters failed to get even an interview. Concerned about embarking on the course with no training place, he visited a careers fair with a friend and found himself drawn to retail work.

'I'd always been interested in finance and enjoyed accountancy work and at the fair I attended a seminar run by Marks & Spencer. The company was excellent, the financial manager role was interesting and the pay good, so I decided to apply.'

As a management trainee Peter spent nine months in Ilford and nine more in Romford, to become familiar with financial, personnel and commercial aspects of the job. He worked alongside supervisors and undertook special projects, such as running a Christmas gift shop, before being made Assistant Financial Manager in Peterborough and then in Norwich, in charge of banking, security, cash control, auditing and cash accounting.

At this point the company was restructured and Peter became Store Manager at King's Lynn and was then offered a promotion to Facilities Manager, based at the Lakeside Thurrock branch and looking after the buildings, environment, health and safety and contractors at Thurrock, Basildon, Brentwood and Southend.

After 18 months he was made Head of Retail Operations based in Middlesbrough in charge of five stores in the north east. After Marks & Spencer underwent another restructuring Peter has recently been appointed Commercial Manager Store Operations in Watford.

Looking back Peter feels his law degree has been helpful in his retail career: 'I thoroughly enjoyed the course. I think that being a mature student and starting my degree at 22 meant I could relate a lot of its content to real life and find it made sense. I've also got a memory like an elephant, which is a help!

'Today my legal background means I can pick up on points and understand legal implications of issues such as health and safety and negligence and the need to act quickly and gather evidence.'

Peter's profile shows clearly how his legal studies have helped him to develop the skills required for a successful career in retail.

Social work and the probation service 12

Social work

Social workers support people who have problems and who sometimes have reached crisis point, helping them to make crucial decisions and to regain control of their lives.

A strong interest in people is vital for a career in social work, but that in itself isn't enough. The career demands a great deal more and many of the qualities it requires link closely with those gained by studying for a law degree. Knowledge of how the law works is important because it helps to ensure that any advice given is appropriate.

Social workers need to be:

★ quick thinking
★ flexible in their approach
★ good communicators
★ able to relate to people who are coping with difficult situations
★ able to cope emotionally with hostility and anger
★ good listeners
★ patient, able to help people make their own decisions
★ able to work in a team with other professionals such as teachers, doctors, lawyers and the police
★ well organised
★ efficient time managers.

The work is demanding and requires many of the skills gained through a law degree including flexibility, self-confidence, teamwork, strong organisational skills.

Starting salaries for social workers and probation staff are in the region of £12,000.

What can I do with... a law degree?

The jobs

Some of a social worker's responsibilities are set down by law.
These include protecting people who are at risk. This could
mean making sure that children are not being brought up in an
environment where they suffer from abuse or neglect, or
ensuring that a person who is suffering from a mental health
problem is not likely to be a danger to him or herself or to
other people.

Many social workers are employed in the social services
departments of a local authority, but there are plenty of other
openings, such as:

★ education departments and special schools
★ residential care homes
★ day centres
★ drop-in and community projects
★ NHS trusts, hospitals
★ health care teams, GP practices
★ youth justice teams and projects
★ charities.

Different types of social work are divided into broad areas,
although most social workers will work with several different
user-groups during the course of their careers.

Work with children and young people

Around half of all social workers are employed in this area and
their first concern is to make sure that children are safe and
secure. Opportunities include the following:

Residential work – most children who are looked after by a
local authority are in foster care, but for some this is not an
option. Residential social workers oversee the daily activities
of children in residential care, assessing their needs and
offering individual support. In some cases they help the

children to maintain contact with family members and to prepare for the time they leave care and live independently. Residential social workers spend some nights sleeping in and also work shifts including evenings and weekends.

Educational welfare and social work – deals with problems that prevent children and young people from making the most of educational opportunities. Social workers become involved when schools are concerned about a pupil's progress, behaviour or attendance.

Work with children and families – social services departments are required by law to identify and protect children who may be at risk of harm. In most cases this means helping them and their families to cope with their problems and stay together. When this support is not enough social workers, together with other professionals, such as doctors and teachers, may decide that a child should be removed from home.

Adoption and fostering – if children cannot remain at home they need fostering or adoptive homes. Social workers interview possible foster carers or adoptive parents to make sure they are suitable and train, advise and support them when a child is placed in their home.

Hospital social work – coping with children who are sick or in some cases dying can be extremely distressing for families, which is why some children's wards employ social workers to offer support.

Work with adults

This is divided into two areas: care management – organising the care, and care provision – working directly with people who need support.

Care managers assess users' needs themselves and also take into account assessments carried out by other professionals such as occupational therapists and GPs. They then discuss with the professionals and the individuals who are to receive the care what support will be provided. It is the care manager who sets up the care package and makes sure it is delivered. This involves keeping computerised records and having financial information.

Care providers' work covers several areas:

Health care social work takes place in a health service setting such as a hospital, GP practice, accident and emergency unit or psychiatric unit. The work involves supporting patients and organising care in the community after they leave.

Forensic social work is based in hospitals such as Rampton or Broadmoor and involves working with people with serious mental health problems who have committed criminal offences.

Residential care work offers support to small groups of people, helping them to live as independently as possible within a sheltered community. This could mean working in a hostel or house, supporting people with learning difficulties or mental health problems, helping them budget, cope with daily tasks and develop a social life.

Day care – many people who are elderly or have mental health problems or learning disabilities benefit from day care services. Social workers in this area help people to develop social contacts, improve or relearn skills they have lost and provide a chance to talk over problems.

Getting in

Work experience is important and can be gained through voluntary work, carried out in the evening or at weekends and holidays.

Graduates who can show evidence of an interest in social work can apply to join a two-year postgraduate DipSW programme run at universities and colleges across the UK. Some bursaries are available to help with the financial cost of training and part-time courses are available so it is possible to have a job and gain a qualification at the same time.

The probation service

Probation officers work with offenders from their first court appearance to the time they complete their sentence. The aim of their work is to cut down the rate of reoffending and protect the public.

In addition to the qualities needed by all social workers, probation officers particularly have to get on with people of all ages and backgrounds and be able to cope with difficult situations and aggressive attitudes. It is very demanding work and requires to a high degree those qualities needed by all social workers, many of which have been gained by law graduates as a result of their studies.

The jobs

Probation officers work in criminal courts giving advice on sentencing options; in prisons with prisoners trying to change the attitudes that have led them to commit crimes; and in the community with offenders who have been given rehabilitation and community punishment orders.

Court work – probation officers write pre-sentence reports in which they look at the offender and the crime, assess the likelihood of reoffending and consider which of a range of sentences would be suitable. In some cases instead of writing a report probation officers give a shorter verbal report at the time a case is heard.

Prison work – risk assessments are carried out on prisoners being considered for release and those awaiting trial. Probation officers work with prison staff in helping prisoners to manage their sentences, working for example with small groups and giving support to individuals.

Community – prisoners report to their probation officer immediately after release and at regular intervals during their supervision period. The probation officer draws up a supervision plan, which covers issues such as housing, employment and fitting back into life in the community.

Not all offenders receive a prison sentence. Many are given community rehabilitation orders (previously probation orders). These run between six months and three years, during which time offenders report regularly to a probation officer and take part in a supervision plan aimed at preventing further offences.

Community punishment orders can run alongside rehabilitation orders and are also supervised by a probation officer. The orders are often made for offences against the community, for example criminal damage, and involve work such as gardening, decorating or removing graffiti from public buildings.

Getting in

A degree in law together with subjects such as sociology and psychology are particularly suited to a career in the probation service.

Previous relevant work experience, usually in the form of voluntary work, is essential. Professional training leads to the Diploma in Probation Studies (DipPS). This two-year training combines academic teaching and work-based supervised practice.

In Scotland probation work is carried out through local authority social services departments, and in Scotland and

Northern Ireland a social work qualification is the way into the probation service.

Tony Foy
Senior Probation Officer, Highgate Office, Harringay Division, London Probation Area

A-levels: pure maths, applied maths, statistics, physics
Degree: BA Law and Politics, Bournemouth University
MA and CQSW (social work qualification), Leicester University

Tony heads a team of probation officers, working closely with the police to prevent further offending and to protect the public. This includes the supervision of convicted offenders with a high risk of harm to the public. In this group are potentially dangerous individuals who have committed violent and sexual offences.

High risk offenders are usually seen on a weekly basis and where appropriate they are linked to relevant programmes to help them to modify their behaviour.

In Tony's words, 'It's a difficult and demanding job and given the type of offenders we work with it's not easy for the public to understand what we do. I think that's something we need to change.

'However I still enjoy my work and while it's not easy to measure success, when offenders do change the pattern of their lives, the feeling of satisfaction lasts a long time.'

After A-levels Tony read engineering for a year at London University before deciding it wasn't for him. He went on to gain a law degree and during the course found he was particularly interested in social welfare legislation.

After graduation he worked as a volunteer with the Citizens Advice Bureau before taking a job with the probation service. When offered the option to study for an MA and a social work qualification at Leicester University, Tony was still considering whether to continue legal training and become a solicitor.

What can I do with... a law degree?

Eventually he decided to go to Leicester and, after his studies, returned to London and the probation service.

Working with people who are involved with the legal system, Tony's law degree has proved an asset in his work.

In his words, 'I spend a lot of time in court and I'm in close contact with solicitors. Studying law has meant I can cut through stuff that isn't relevant and reach the heart of an issue. It's also given me a good understanding of legal terms and systems and means I'm not phased by "legal speak".

Valuable legal knowledge, together with a logical, objective approach to the job, and the ability to see through to the central issues – skills that Tony feels he gained from his legal studies.

Police and prison services **13**

The police

Every year well over six million emergency calls are made to the police, and as the work becomes more complex so does the need to find the right kind of recruits who are able to deal with the demands of the job.

In England and Wales the police service is divided into 43 forces. There are 8 forces in Scotland, and there is the Police Service of Northern Ireland.

Skills needed for a career in the police are:

★ good communication skills
★ the ability to work with people from all backgrounds and of all ages
★ the ability to work as part of a team
★ leadership qualities, being able to take the initiative when necessary
★ strong observation skills
★ a good memory
★ physical courage and fitness to confront violent situations
★ emotional resources to face abuse and to break bad news
★ good colour vision (most forces accept candidates who wear glasses or contact lenses).

The police stress that they are not looking for graduates with degrees in any particular subject, many of the qualities they are looking for in recruits are those gained during legal studies. These include communication skills, teamwork and leadership qualities.

Starting salary for a trainee police officer is around £18,264, rising to around £20,436 after basic training.

The job

All new recruits to the police force undergo the same training for the first two years. Every recruit becomes a probationary constable, with the first few weeks spent at a local training centre followed by three to four months at a national training centre. Subjects studied include law (which law graduates would not find difficult) self-defence and understanding the criminal mind. Then it's back to the station and on to the beat with an experienced officer. The next step is the sergeants' examination, which has two parts – the written and the practical.

There are a number of specialist branches in the police force, such as:

★ The Traffic Department
★ Criminal Investigation Department (CID)
★ Fraud Squad
★ Crime Prevention.

It is not possible to join a specialist branch directly, nor to work exclusively in one particular area. Promotion usually means moving to and from departments in order to gain a wide experience of police work.

Getting in

Graduates can enter the force both by the standard route and the High Potential Development scheme. No particular degree subjects are specified. Rather than academic ability, the police are looking for very particular qualities in their recruits.

The High Potential Development scheme aims to seek out individuals with the potential to be the future leaders of the police service and to help them realise their potential through an individually tailored career development programme. It is not restricted to graduates nor to those at the beginning of their careers. It recognises that people develop at different rates and at different stages.

Once selected on to the scheme officers follow their own tailored career development process, designed around their own particular needs. The training is modular and students undertake those sections that will help them to perform better on the job. There is also an academic element, which gives students an opportunity to gain at least a Master's level qualification.

Chris Noble
Inspector, Police Service of Northern Ireland

A-levels: English literature, politics, history
Degree: LLB, Queen's University Belfast

'When I started my degree course I hoped to specialise in criminal law, but I soon realised that in Northern Ireland the criminal law sector is saturated with lawyers and I needed to think again.'

As Chris's course progressed he found that the parts he particularly enjoyed were the practical applications of the law, which suit his personality and his hands-on approach.

At the end of his second year he applied to what was then the Royal Ulster Constabulary and is now the Police Service of Northern Ireland and was accepted as a standard entrant. At the end of his first year after 'a gruelling three and a half days' interview', Chris went on to the Accelerated Promotion Scheme.

He explains, 'The first two years' training is the same for everyone, which I think is important, because basically you have to want to be a police officer. I spent this time at Castlereagh Police Station in Belfast, dealing with the traffic accidents and domestic incidents, which make up the day-to-day work of any police force.

'Being a police officer you are often the first point of contact for people in crisis who are at their most vulnerable. The way you treat them does have a positive impact and it's important to remember this.'

After passing his sergeants' exams Chris went to work with the Policing Review team. As a result of the Patten Report, which recommended changes to the police service in Northern Ireland, a number of projects were set up in the province and Chris's job was to track the effects these were having within the service.

In his words, 'After being on the beat, I was suddenly working at a strategic level and could see at first hand how change takes place.'

After two years Chris moved again, this time to be a uniformed sergeant at Mountpottinger Police Station in Belfast. He describes this move as 'a chance to take responsibility for personnel issues and on the ground decisions at an "interface" station, bordering on both nationalist and loyalist areas in Belfast'.

After two years at Mountpottinger, Chris was promoted to the rank of inspector and took up a post with the Parades Commission. In Northern Ireland the traditional marches, usually of loyalists through nationalist areas, have long been a source of tension. The loyalist marchers see the parades as part of their history, while the nationalists regard them as provocative.

The Parades Commission examines applications to parade and recommends either that the march can go ahead, that it be rerouted or in some cases that it be banned. Chris explains, 'My work involved carrying out a risk analysis on the possible outcome of particular marches and reporting back to the Commission so they could bear the information in mind when making a judgement.'

He has now moved again and at present is Sector Commander in Carrickfergus, 'an area with a strong paramilitary presence, where for some time threats have been made to the Roman Catholic population, so dealing with sectarian tensions plays a large part in policing duties in the area'.

Chris feels that having a law degree has been helpful in a number of ways. 'People have a lot of respect for a law degree and while in my work I only use a small part of the legal topics I studied at university, there is no doubt that the skills I learned there help me everyday.

'My studies helped me to be self-motivated and most importantly to be analytical in my approach, to be able to lift relevant strands of information from a large body of facts.'

The prison service

The prison service is going through a period of change at present, with some prisons now being managed by private companies.

Inside a prison some prisoners will be on remand, which means they are awaiting trial, while others have been tried and are serving their sentences. Sentenced prisoners are given a category from A to D and this decides the type of prison to which they are sent. Category A prisoners are the highest security prisoners who are regarded as a danger to society and they spend part or all of their sentences in top security prisons. At the other end of the scale, Category D prisoners are trusted not to escape. Most of them are in open prisons working in the community. There are also juvenile young offender institutions for those under 21.

Prison work is not easy. Many prisoners go on to offend again and a prison population will include men and women who will be in prison for long periods of time, or for life, those who regularly try to harm themselves, sex offenders and drug addicts. The prison service has a number of courses prisoners can take to help them not to reoffend and offers support to all prisoners regardless of their crime.

Prison managers and governors need particular qualities:

★ the ability to relate positively to prisoners and to treat them with the respect every human being deserves

What can I do with... a law degree?

* ★ a strong interest in social problems
* ★ enthusiasm and integrity
* ★ good organisational skills
* ★ leadership skills
* ★ tact, firmness
* ★ the ability to motivate others
* ★ a sense of humour
* ★ a reasonable level of physical fitness and good eyesight.

Again many of these mirror the skills gained through legal studies.

Principal officers earn around £29,000, which can rise to around £60,000 for the most senior governors.

The job

Prisons are managed by governors, who are responsible for security, staff, prisoner care and resources. They organise the work and training of prison officers, maintain prison records, deal with disciplinary matters and requests for parole and carry out risk assessments on prisoners.

Governors supervise prisoner development and work closely with other professionals such as chaplains, psychiatrists and probation officers. A senior governor is in charge of a prison and working with him or her is a team of governor grade staff.

Getting in

The prison service runs a Fast Track scheme for graduates who show themselves to be capable of moving from prison officer to management status within five years. It is open to all graduates, but law is one of the subjects listed as being particularly helpful for a career in the prison service.

New recruits on the Fast Track scheme spend an induction week at the Prison Service College followed by a week's observation in a prison before going back to college for nine weeks' initial training followed by a nine-month posting as a prison officer.

The next step is the prison officer's promotion exams and those who pass move on to a three-week management development course to prepare them for a promotion assessment to principal officer. Once promoted they move to a different prison for 12 months, working at the higher grade with responsibility for a group of staff and for running a part of the organisation such as the residential wing.

At the end of this time officers are assessed for promotion to operational manager (governor grade) level and when this happens they undergo a further month's training followed by two placements, each lasting a year. The second placement includes responsibility for staff supervision, prisoner care and development and for managing part of a prison establishment.

When this period is complete, officers are eligible for promotion to functional head, which is a senior management position.

Both the police and the prison services are looking for a particular type of graduate: well organised, professional in approach, young people with leadership qualities who enjoy working as part of a team. These are essentially the qualities gained by legal graduates.

14 The beginning not the end

The majority of the profile subjects in this book set off to university with a clear career plan or route map. Some of them have followed this route and achieved the goals they had set themselves, but others are now enjoying careers that they would not have considered at the beginning of their law studies.

Some realised during their studies that they were interested in a particular aspect of the law. Chris Noble, now a police inspector, discovered he was interested in its practical application, while Gail Sanderson, a director of information services, found that it was law in the abstract which appealed to her. Mark Winter, senior director of a bank and Stephanie Russon, publisher, took temporary jobs for financial reasons, only to find these opened up new and exciting areas of opportunity.

Flexibility

Planning for a future career is vital, and nothing beats work experience for a clear picture of what a job is really like. Camilla Tominey, the journalist, warmed to the atmosphere of the newspaper office as quickly as she formed a dislike for the legal offices she visited. However, just as forward planning and preparation are important, so is flexibility. Setting targets and goals is a sound idea, but so is being aware of doors opening and offering something new.

Nobody can say with complete certainty exactly what the future holds. Today there is a growing trend for people to have more than one career, to embark on new studies, gain further qualifications and move from one area of work to another. The chosen career at 20 may not be what you want at 30 or 40 or 50.

Over and over again the legal graduates profiled in the book list the same skills they feel they gained from taking a law degree and that they feel are a great asset to them in their careers, whatever these may be. These skills are:

★ analytical – 'the ability to cut through the waffle'
★ problem solving
★ communication
★ attention to detail
★ self-confidence
★ team working
★ leadership.

The profiles all felt that they owed a great deal to their law studies and had a certain pride and confidence in succeeding in a subject which is widely regarded as one of the most demanding.

You may finish a law degree and feel less certain of your future career than you did when you started, but you will have gained in strong measure the qualities needed to succeed in a wide range of different careers.

From a practical point of view you will also have a qualification that could enable you to earn a decent living while you consider your future!

During his studies Anthony Jucha saw himself as a lawyer. After a short time with a legal firm he was struck by wanderlust and the urge to write about his travels. At that point he realised the full value of his law degree.

Anthony Jucha
Lawyer
Degree: Law and Economics, Adelaide University
　　　　　Graduate Certificate in Legal Practice, University of
　　　　　South Australia

After gaining a professional legal qualification in Australia Anthony worked for Finlaysons, a major commercial law firm in

Adelaide, for two years, before leaving to set up an IT company with friends. He helped to finance this venture by taking a short-term contract with a legal firm in Darwin.

In his words, 'It was a small firm dealing with some large litigation so it needed to take on extra staff for a few months and that suited me well.'

Anthony left the IT start-up to take another placement, this time for nine months in the legal department of FH Faulding & Co. Ltd, an international pharmaceutical company.

'I'd never had a gap year and I liked the notion of travelling and writing. I could see that my legal qualification could be the way to fund my ambition, while giving me valuable experience in different legal areas.'

After saving hard Anthony set off for India for six months where he found plenty to see and write about. When money grew tight he came to London, and with his working holiday visa took a three-month contract with a brand management company, which was restructuring its legal department.

Anthony explains: 'There are good opportunities for Australian lawyers in the UK and for UK lawyers in Australia. The two legal systems are very similar, one simply has to be careful about checking legislation.'

His next contract lasted nine months and was with Shell International Ltd, covering maternity leave and dealing with issues arising from service station franchises in the UK. Anthony was offered a chance to stay on, but by this time he had enough money to fund his next adventure.

As World Cup fever hit the globe, Anthony was off visiting the 13 European countries in the competition and posting reports of his adventures to www.abctales.com, a non-profit writers' website that donates 20 per cent of its revenue to *The Big Issue*. He then went on to spend another three months in Europe before returning to Adelaide.

He says, 'I see my law degree as empowering me to do what I want. It has given me skills in argument, critical thinking and writing and opened a lot of doors. As far as I'm concerned the future is wide open. I could do more short-term contract work. I could join a legal department in a large organisation or opt for a job with a small legal firm. I could set up my own business, or continue travelling and writing about my adventures.'

The future is wide open

Whatever you choose to do with it, a law degree is a valuable and a marketable qualification and there has possibly never been a more exciting time to embark on a legal career.

As a young lawyer, working on everyday legal cases in Brazil, Edesio Fernandes had little idea of the direction his career would take. His interest in environmental issues, concern for justice to be accessible to all, plus a belief in that most basic of human rights – the right to a home – have led him to his present legal advisory role to governments across the world.

Edesio Fernandes
Environmental consultant, university lecturer

Degree: LLM, PhD, Warwick University

Edesio studied law at university in Brazil and after graduation trained to become a lawyer. (Brazilian lawyers are not divided into solicitors and barristers/advocates as in the UK.)

He practised as a lawyer for several years, doing some lecturing at the same time. Along with the usual cases undertaken by most lawyers, he carried out some city planning work for the state administration authority, which helped to develop his interest in environmental work.

To further his knowledge of environmental issues Edesio won a British Council Scholarship to study for a LLM Master's level degree at Warwick University. He says, 'What appealed to me about the course at Warwick was the inter-disciplinary approach which included sociology, politics and economics. At that time such a course was not available in Brazil.'

In fact Edesio's studies in Warwick were postponed for two years. 'From 1964 to 1986 Brazil was governed by a military dictatorship. When democracy was restored the country needed to reconstruct its entire legal system and I was asked to act as legal adviser to the newly elected assembly.'

Edesio extended his time at Warwick in order to complete his PhD, and while he was there he was contacted by a South African who had read one of his papers and was struck by similarities between the situations in South Africa and Brazil. As a result of this contact Edesio became an adviser to the African National Congress.

In 1993 he set up Law and Urban Space, an international network of lawyers involved with urban development planning. From fewer than 10 members it now has more than 150 and is recognised by the United Nations.

Today Edesio is based in London but travels the globe. He undertakes projects in Brazil two or three times a year. He has recently worked in Albania and at present is in discussion with the Kosovan government on how to approach planning issues in line with social reforms and the country's application for membership of the European Union.

Working in so many different countries, he believes that once you step beyond traditional boundaries legal systems often have a great deal in common.

'Solutions to problems might take different forms in different countries but basically they are similar and becoming more so. In England the traditional legal system is not written down. It is based on precedence, or cases that have gone before. However, life is more complicated than it used to be and today this system is supported more and more by acts passed by Parliament. Equally in Brazil, where laws are written down, a broader approach than before is taken towards their judicial interpretation.

Edesio sees problems developing within legal systems that will have to be tackled. He explains, 'A growing problem is that of law enforcement. There is no point in having laws if they cannot be enforced, which is the case in many developing countries.

'There is also the question of illegality and what it means. In some countries between 40 per cent and 80 per cent of the population live illegally on land they have been forced to invade in order to stay alive. Then there is the matter of access to justice. Many people even in developed countries such as the UK are denied the right to justice in the courts because the procedure is too lengthy and too expensive.'

Edesio has moved from his early career as a lawyer in Brazil, when he was concerned with the application of laws, to being involved with the law-making process.

He is one of a growing number of lawyers equipped to take a global view of legal systems and to use his knowledge to benefit disadvantaged groups in all parts of the world.

'The fascinating thing about the law is that it's always changing.' These were the words of Eleanor Robinson, solicitor. How right she is!

Young people are now working in legal areas that would have been beyond the imagination of lawyers 50 years ago and these opportunities are still growing, as legal systems change and develop to meet the needs of today.

Equally, as the profiles within these pages show, a legal qualification is the beginning and not the end. It is proof of impressive academic achievement, just as important is that it can lead to the development of the life skills you need to tackle whatever lies ahead.

15 Useful addresses

The legal profession

The Bar Council
3 Bedford Row
London WC1R 4DB
Tel: 020 7691 8900
Website: www.barcouncil.org.uk

The Bar Council of Northern Ireland
PO Box 414
Royal Courts of Justice
Chichester Street
Belfast BT1 3JP
Tel: 028 90 56 2349
Website: www.barcouncil-ni-org.uk
Email: administration@barcouncil-ni.org.uk

Faculty of Advocates
11 Parliament House
Edinburgh EH1 1RF
Tel: 0131 226 5071
Website: www.advocates.org.uk

GLS (Government Legal Service) Recruitment Team
Queen Anne's Chambers
28 Broadway
London SW1H 9JS
Tel: 020 7210 3304
Website: www.gls.gov.uk
Email: recruit@gls.gsi.gov.uk

The Institute of Legal Executives
Kempston Manor

Kempston
Bedford MK42 7AB
Tel: 01234 841000
Website: www.ilex.org.uk
Email: info@ilex.org.uk

The Institute of Professional Legal Studies
10 Lennoxvale
Malone Road
Belfast BT9 5BY
Tel: 028 90 335566
Website: www.qub.ac.uk/ipls

The Law Society
Ipsley Court
Berrington Close
Redditch B98 0TD
Tel: 020 7242 1222
Website: www.training.lawsociety.org.uk

The Law Society of Northern Ireland
Law Society House
98 Victoria Street
Belfast BT1 3JZ
Tel: 028 90 231614
Website: www.lawsoc-ni.org
Email: info@lawsoc-ni.org

The Law Society of Scotland
26 Drumsheugh Gardens
Edinburgh EH3 7YR
Tel: 0131 226 7411
Website: www.lawscot.org.uk
Email: lawscot@lawscot.org.uk

The Recruitment Branch
Crown Prosecution Service
50 Ludgate Hill

What can I do with... a law degree?

London EC4M 7EX
Tel: 020 7796 8053
Website: www.cps.gov.uk

The Recruitment Unit
The Scottish Executive
T Spur
Saughton House
Broomhouse Drive
Edinburgh EH11 3XD
Tel: 0131 244 3964
Website: www.scotland.gov.uk/government/careers

Finance

Accountancy

The Association of Chartered Certified Accountants
Student Promotions
29 Lincoln's Inn Fields
London WC2A 3EE
Tel: 020 7396 5700
Website: www.accaglobal.com

The Association of International Accountants
South Bank Building
Kingsway
Team Valley
Newcastle upon Tyne NE11 0JS
Tel: 0191 482 4409
Website: www.aia.org.uk
Email: aia@aia.org.uk

The Chartered Institute of Public Finance and Accountancy
3 Robert Street
London
WC2N 6RL
Tel: 020 7543 5600
Website: www.cipfa.org.uk

The Chartered Institute of Management Accountants
26 Chapter Street
London SW1P 4NP
Tel: 020 7663 5441
Website: www.cimaglobal.com
Email: student.services@cimaglobal.com

The Institute of Chartered Accountants in England and Wales
Gloucester House
399 Silbury Boulevard
Central Milton Keynes MK9 2HL
Tel: 01908 248108
Website: www.icaew.co.uk/careers
Email: studentsupport@icaew.co.uk

The Institute of Chartered Accountants in Scotland
Student Education Department
C A House
21 Haymarket Yard
Edinburgh EH12 5BH
Tel: 0131 347 0100
Website: www.icas.org.uk
Email: enquiries@icas.org.uk

Banking

The Chartered Institute of Bankers in Scotland
Drumsheugh House
38B Drumsheugh Gardens
Edinburgh EH3 7SW
Tel: 0131 473 7777
Website: www.ciobs.org.uk
Email: info@ciobs.org.uk

The Institute of Financial Services
IFS House
4–9 Burgate Lane
Canterbury
Kent CT1 2XJ

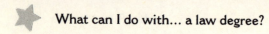

Tel: 01227 818609
Website: www.ifslearning.com
Email: customerservices@ifslearning.com

Insurance

The British Insurance Brokers Association
14 Bevis Marks
London EC3A 7NT
Tel: 020 7623 9043
Website: www.biba.org.uk

The Chartered Insurance Institute
20 Aldermanbury
London EC2V 7HY
Tel: 020 7417 4793
Website: www.cii.co.uk

The Stock Exchange

Financial Services Authority
25 The North Colonnade
Canary Wharf
London E14 5HS
Tel: 020 7676 1000
Website: www.fsa.gov.uk
Email: enquiries@fsa.gov.uk

Publicity Information Department
The London Stock Exchange
Old Broad Street
London EC2N 1HP
Tel: 020 7797 1372
Website: www.londonstockexchange.com
Email: enquiries@londonstockexchange.com

Civil Service, local government, administration

Capita RAS
Innovation Court

New Street
Basingstoke
Hampshire RG21 7JB
Tel: 01256 383780
Website: www.capitaras.co.uk

The Institute of Chartered Secretaries and Administrators
16 Park Crescent
London W1B 1AH
Tel: 020 7580 4741
Website: www.icsa.org.uk
Email: info@icsa.co.uk

MM Group Ltd
Unit 2–4 Lescren Way
Avonmouth
Bristol BS11 8DG
Tel: 0117 982 1171
Email: ship.shape@btinternet.com

Personnel or human resources

The Chartered Institute of Personnel and Development
CIPD House
35 Camp Road
Wimbledon
London SW19 4UX
Tel: 020 8971 9000
Website: www.cipd.co.uk
Email: cipd@cipd.co.uk

Library and information management

Aslib The Association for Information Management
Temple Chambers
3–7 Temple Avenue
London EC4Y 0HP
Tel: 020 7583 8900

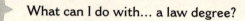

Website: www.aslib.com
Email: aslib@aslib.com

Chartered Institute of Library and Information Professionals
(formerly Library Association)
7 Ridgmount Street
London WC1E 7AE
Tel: 020 7255 0500
Website: www.cilip.org.uk
Email: info@cilip.org.uk

Information technology

British Computer Society
1 Sanford Street
Swindon SN1 1HJ
Tel: 01793 417417
Website: www.bcs.org

e-skills uk
1 Castle Lane
London SW1E 6DR
Tel: 020 7963 8920
Website: www.e-skills.com
Email: info@e-skills.com

Journalism and publishing

Journalism

Broadcast Journalism Training Council
18 Millers Close
Ripingdale
Nr Bourne
Lincolnshire PE10 0TH
Tel: 01778 440025
Website: www.bjtc.org.uk

National Council for the Training of Journalists
Latton Bush Centre

Southern Way
Harlow
Essex CM18 7BL
Tel: 01279 430009
Website: www.nctj.com
Email: info@nctj.com

Periodicals Training Council
55–56 Lincoln's Inn Fields
London WC2A 3LJ
Tel: 020 7400 7509
Website: www.ppa.co.uk/ptc
Email: training@ppa.co.uk

Publishing

Institute of Publishing
Hamilton Court
Gogmore Lane
Chertsey KT16 9AP
Tel: 01932 571932
Website: www.instpublishing.org.uk

London College of Printing
Elephant and Castle
London SE1 6SB
Tel: 020 7514 6514
Website: www.lcp.linst.ac.uk
Email: info@lcp.linst.ac.uk

London School of Publishing and Public Relations
David Game House
69 Notting Hill Gate
London W11 3JS
Tel: 020 7221 3399
Website: www.publishing-school.co.uk or
Website: www.pr-school-london.com
Email: lsp@easynet.co.uk

Publishers Association
29b Montague Street
London WC1B 5BH
Tel: 020 7691 9191
Website: www.publishers.org.uk
Email: mail@publishers.org.uk

The Publishing Training Centre
Book House
45 East Hill
Wandsworth
London SW18 2QZ
Tel: 020 8874 2718
Website: www.train4publishing.co.uk

Society for Editors and Proofreaders (SfEP)
Riverbank House
1 Putney Bridge Approach
Fulham
London SW6 3JD
Tel: 020 7736 3278
Website: www.sfep.org.uk
Email: administration@sfep.org.uk

Society of Young Publishers (SYP)
c/o Endeavour House
189 Shaftesbury Avenue
London WC2H 8TJ
Website: www.thesyp.org.uk

Advertising and marketing

Marketing

The Chartered Institute of Marketing
Moor Hall
Cookham
Maidenhead

Berkshire SL6 9QH
Tel: 01628 427500
Website: www.cim.co.uk
Email: marketing@cim.co.uk

The Institute of Export
Export House
Minerva Business Park
Lynchwood
Peterborough PE2 6FT
Tel: 01733 404400
Website: www.export.org.uk
Email: institute@export.org.uk

Advertising

The CAM Foundation
Moor Hall
Cookham
Maidenhead
Berkshire SWV 1NJ
Tel: 01628 427180
Website: www.camfoundation.com
Email: info@camfoundation.com

Institute of Practitioners in Advertising
44 Belgrave Square
London SW1X 8QS
Tel: 020 7235 7020
Website: www.ipa.co.uk
Email: info@ipa.co.uk

Retail

British Shops and Stores Association (BSSA)
Middleton House
2 Main Road
Middleton Cheney

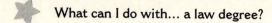

Banbury OX17 2TN
Tel: 01295 712277
Website: www.british-shops.co.uk
Email: info@bssa.co.uk

CSIA
Fraser House
Nether Hall Road
Doncaster DN1 2PH
Tel: 01302 380000
Website: www.csia.net or
www.habia.org.uk
Email: mail@csia.net

Distributive Industries Training Advisory Council
Middleton House
2 Main Road
Middleton Cheney
Banbury OX17 2TN
Tel: 01295 712277
Website: www.di-net.co.uk
Email: admin@ditac.org.uk

Social work

Care Council for Wales
6th Floor
West Wing
Southgate House
Wood Street
Cardiff CF10 1EW
Tel: 029 2022 6257
Website: www.ccwales.org.uk
Email: info@ccwales.org.uk

General Social Care Council
Goldings House

2 Hays Lane
London SE1 2HB
Tel: 020 7397 5100
Website: www.socialworkcareers.co.uk or
www.gscc.org.uk
The National Youth Agency
17–23 Albion Street
Leicester LE1 6GD
Tel: 0116 285 3792
Email: dutydesk@nya.org.uk

Northern Ireland Social Care Council
7th Floor
Millennium House
Great Victoria Street
Belfast BT2 7AQ
Tel: 028 9041 7600
Website: www.niscc.info
Email: info@niscc.n-i.nhs.uk

Scottish Social Services Council
Compass House
Discovery Quay
Riverside Drive
Dundee DD1 4NY
Tel: 08456 030891
Website: www.carecommission.com
Email: info-scotland@sssc.uk.com

Police

High Potential Development Scheme
Fifth Floor Tower
Room 548
H M Inspectorate of Constabulary, Personnel &
Administration
Home Office

50 Queen Anne's Gate
London SW1H 9AT
Tel: 020 7273 3000 or 0870 000 1585

The Police Service of Northern Ireland
Brooklyn
65 Knock Road
Belfast BT5 6LE
Tel: 028 9065 0222
Website: www.psni.police.uk

The Scottish Police College
Tulliallan Castle
Kincardine
Alloa FK10 4BE
Tel: 01259 732000

Prison service

The Fast Track Scheme Team
HM Prison Service
Room 329
Cleland House
Page Street
London SW1P 4LN
Tel: 020 7217 6437

Probation service

National Association of Probation Officers
3–4 Chivalry Road
London SW11 1HT
Tel: 020 7223 4887
Email: info@napo.org.uk

Probation Training Unit
Mitre House

223–237 Borough High Street
London SE1 1JD
Tel: 020 7740 8500
Website: www.probation-london.org.uk